Baby Number Three

By Tamara Chavalle

 A catalogue record for this book is available from the National Library of Australia

Copyright © 2024 by Leanne Poole

All rights reserved, including the right to reproduce this book or portions thereof in any form whatsoever.

Publisher:
Australian Self Publishing Group, Pty. Ltd / Inspiring Publishers
PO Box 159, Calwell, ACT 2905, Australia.
Phone: 61-(0) 2 6291-2904
http://australianselfpublishinggroup.com

National Library of Australia Prepublication Data Service

Author: Tamara Chavalle

Title: **Baby Number Three**

ISBN: 978-1-923250-32-1 (print)
ISBN: 978-1-923250-33-8 (ePub2)
ISBN: 978-1-923250-34-5 (Hardcover)

Dedication

Mum. Thank you for your unwavering
support and belief in me, no matter what.

My babies, you make me want to be the best version
of myself. When times get tough your faces drive me
to keep pushing forward.

And Alex Munroe, my wonderful Editor and friend.
You ask me to do things I didn't know I was capable of.
I truly appreciate you.

Table of Contents

Dedication 3

Chapter 1 : Early January 2023 7

Chapter 2 : Mid-January 2023 15

Chapter 3 : Mid-January 2023 Continued.................................22

Chapter 4 : Late January 2023 28

Chapter 5 : February 2023 37

Chapter 6 : Early March 2023 42

Chapter 7 : 21st March 2023 46

Chapter 8 : Late March 2023 55

Chapter 9 : April 2023.. 67

Chapter 10 : May 2023..77

Chapter 11 : Late May 2023 88

Chapter 12 : A week later 93

Chapter 13 : June 2023 105

Chapter 14 : June 2023 - Continued 111

Chapter 15 : July 2023 118

Chapter 16 : August 2023 124

Chapter 17 : September 2023 135

Chapter 18 : December 2023 139

Chapter 19 : Mid-December 2023 147

Chapter 20 : Christmas 2023 153

Chapter 21 : New Year's Eve 2023 158

Chapter 22 : 1st January 2024 161

Chapter 23 : 14th January 2024 169

Chapter 24 : February 2024 176

Chapter 25 : 13th April 2024 183

Chapter 26 : 17th April 2024 189

Chapter 27 : 22nd April 2024 199

Chapter 28 : 23rd April 2024 209

Chapter 29 : August 2024 214

Chapter 1
Early January 2023

I've been ghosted a few times in my life, haven't we all? A couple of years ago, I was even ghosted by a man I was falling in love with. He was a teacher who waited tables every second weekend at a local restaurant for some extra cash. We met when he was working at my mum's 70th birthday party and we hit it off straight away. I'd been single for years, with no interest in a relationship, but something about him intrigued me. We went on our first date a few weeks later and soon became an item.

He was gorgeous, intelligent, and funny. But more importantly, he understood that my child was my number one priority. He had a daughter who was a few years younger than my daughter, Rose. Between our jobs and our kids, we didn't get much time to see each other, but when we did, it was wonderful, blissful, and magical. Our time together was never supposed to be more than a bit of fun—not at first anyway—however, I soon realised that he was exactly the kind of man I could see myself getting serious about and building a life with. But as the weeks passed, I started to feel more and more uncomfortable about something I hadn't told him.

You see, I had been trying to have another baby for almost nine years. I had done numerous rounds of in vitro fertilisation or IVF. I had undergone painful operations to try and flush my tubes and remove endometriosis, all in the hope that I would finally be able to have my longed-for second child.

The day I met him, I was a matter of weeks away from starting a new cocktail of hormones and other medications that would get my body ready to grow a new life within it. The closer I got to starting those medications, the harder I fell for him until eventually, convinced that he would be okay with it, I decided to tell him about my plan. I was sure that we would somehow figure out a way to make it work.

A million different scenarios crossed my mind before and even during the conversation, but I could never have anticipated his response.

"I'll help you!" he exclaimed ever so eagerly.

"Sorry, what do you mean?" I laughed, confused. I was sure that he must have misunderstood me.

"I can get you pregnant easily; I'd be happy to help."

I knew he'd been drinking that evening while he watched the football and chatted with me on the phone, so instead of entertaining his ridiculous offer, I simply changed the subject, assuming that he would forget about it in the morning.

The following night, we went out for dinner at the same Mexican restaurant where we'd had our first date. I had all but forgotten about his unexpected offer to help me have a baby when out of the blue, he started talking about it again.

"You do know I wasn't joking last night, don't you?"

"About what?" I asked, feigning ignorance.

"About helping you have a baby," he replied, looking me straight in the face.

I laughed nervously. "You do realise that at forty-five, there is almost no chance of me getting pregnant naturally, don't you?"

But he was so sure of himself. For the next twenty minutes, we went back and forth as I explained the lengths I'd gone to over the previous nine years and how, even if I did manage to get pregnant, I was unlikely to carry a baby to term without the medications that I was just about to start taking. I felt flattered that he would consider giving me such a precious gift, but once I had finished explaining everything to him, I ordered another round of margaritas before not-so-subtly changing the subject.

For the next few days, we went back and forth, with him insisting on helping me, while I explained over and over that I didn't need, or indeed want, his help. We finally came to an agreement that we would shelve it. He and his daughter were going away with his family for the July school holidays, while

Rose and I had plans to go away with friends, and we didn't want to have anything overshadow our time with our girls.

We spent a wonderful day together before he flew off to Brisbane the next morning, promising to talk whenever we had a chance. He messaged me a couple of times about his flights being delayed that morning. And then nothing. I thought he was just busy with his family at first but as the days passed without so much as an emoji text, the cold, hard fact that I had been ghosted became impossible to ignore.

In the space of a couple of months, I had gone from eternally but happily single to heartbroken. I vowed to myself after that happened that I was never going to get ghosted again. I was never going to put myself in that position again. So imagine my surprise when, just 18 months later, it happened again. This time it was my dream job, well, dream company anyway .

I went ahead with my plan to have another baby, and it worked. I gave birth to my beautiful, healthy little boy Max in May 2022 after almost ten years of fertility treatments. The moment I held him, all the pain and heartache of those years were instantly erased.

Everything was wonderful for a little while. But as the days and weeks passed following Max's birth, it became more apparent that his birth had caused some serious injuries. When he was nine weeks old, I was rushed in for surgery to remove pieces of his placenta that had been left behind, causing a serious infection. A few weeks after that operation, I suffered a severe prolapse of my uterus, bowel, and bladder. My internal organs were just one centimetre from falling out of my body.

As if my health problems weren't enough, I found out, just days after discovering my prolapse, that I was being made redundant from my job, even though I still hadn't returned to work after giving birth to Max. I had been forewarned about the possibility of redundancies from my colleagues. Our company had only been trading in Australia for about a year. The team here had been working tirelessly, but our efforts had not paid off, and the company was not seeing the growth they expected.

There had been talk for weeks about them exiting the market and closing down operations here. I thoroughly enjoyed my sales role with the company, but I couldn't risk being unemployed. That's why, by the time I found out about the fate of my job, I was already in the late stages of interviewing for a new, more senior sales role with another company. The new company, an Australian technology company based in Brisbane, seemed fantastic.

Everyone I spoke with during my interview process was genuinely lovely. I was excited about the challenge of learning everything about the company, the technology, and the team of people I would be working with. But then the doctors confirmed my fears: my prolapsed organs were going to need to be surgically repaired.

I was terrified at the thought of sitting at my desk for eight hours a day when I could barely sit on my lounge. I could barely walk in sneakers, let alone the three-inch heels that I had always worn at work. How on earth was I supposed to carry out a new, highly demanding job when I was so unwell and in so much pain? Thankfully, that new company was understanding when I explained that I was going to need an urgent surgery in November, just a couple of months after I was offered the job.

Without hesitation, they offered the perfect solution. My new boss agreed that there was no point in me starting with them for a month or two and then being out for six weeks to recover from my operation. The job had been newly created because of growth in the sales team, and so he was happy to push my start date out until the end of January the following year. I was thrilled to have such a great plan in place. It was a win-win for everyone.

But the days and weeks that followed my operation were brutal. For weeks, I couldn't even hold my six-month-old baby boy. I was in so much pain, a lot more than I had been during either of my assisted births, even the first one where I had been refused an epidural. If I'd had any understanding of those first few weeks post-op, I doubt that I would ever have gone ahead with the surgery. I would have somehow learnt to live with my injuries. And then, as the weeks passed, I finally started to feel better, but I couldn't shake the nagging feeling that my surgery hadn't worked.

Even six weeks later, when I should have been all patched up and raring to go, I found it hard to sit for more than a few minutes at a time. I also couldn't ignore the terrible impact that looking after my children and I had had on my mum's health. By the time January started, I was in a panic. I wasn't sure how I was going to manage everything on my plate, so I rang the recruiter who had initially put me forward for that new, dream job.

I explained that I wasn't healing as quickly as expected and I asked if there was any way we could push my start date out by another month. Of course, he had no idea what my injuries were or the nature of the surgery I had needed to fix them. I'd learned the hard way many years earlier not to divulge my private, reproductive business to bosses. For all he knew, I could've had a knee reconstruction or a mummy makeover. Either way, he was understanding, asking me to lay out what I had told him in an email to my new boss.

So I did, straight away. I emailed the boss and explained the situation, that I needed a bit more time to recover, while at the same time assuring him that I was still committed to the company and my new role there. I received an almost immediate reply from him, telling me that he understood and we would work it out.

And then the strangest thing happened. Complete and utter silence. Over the next two weeks, I called and emailed both the boss and the recruiter several times. The recruiter had the decency to take my calls but never had any answers. Mr. Nice Guy Boss, on the other hand, had apparently been stranded on a desert island with no phone or internet—or he may as well have been anyway.

Two weeks after that last conversation, I finally realised what had happened. I had been posting and sharing birth trauma information and stories on my LinkedIn page. I had just written a book about those horror months after Max's birth and I was planning to start a podcast because I wanted to join in and elevate the conversation about the horrors that so many women go through during and after childbirth.

I had also opened up about the very real possibility I was facing in order to have my last longed-for baby. You see, my injuries and the surgery to repair my body were very likely going to leave me unable to carry another child. I had started looking into the terrifying reality that I may well need to find a surrogate to help me have that baby.

I had posted the same things on my professional network that I had been posting on my own personal social media accounts. I had done so purely because I felt so passionate about engaging with other women who needed help finding their voices. I felt like I could really help other women like me who had been through so much. But for some reason, that man and the company he worked for had seen my posts as a negative thing and decided that they no longer wanted me to be part of their team.

Strangely, it stung almost as much as it did when it was that guy a year and a half earlier. I couldn't believe that I had been ghosted again, but you know what? I realised something. It was their bloody loss, both times!

Chapter 2
Mid-January 2023

So with all that fuss about the ghostings, I forgot to introduce myself. My name is Tabitha. Tabitha Powell. I'm a single mum with two beautiful children. A thirteen-year-old daughter, that's Rose, and my seven-month-old son, Max. I was forty-six years old when I gave birth to him. That was never part of my plan, to have a baby in my mid-forties, but I so desperately wanted another child that each failed attempt and loss just drove me on, making me more determined to grow my family. I'm glad I persisted because my children are the absolute loves of my life.

We live with my mum, Margaret. She is a kind and selfless woman. Our house has a main residence upstairs, where Mum and my seventeen-year-old niece, Brittany, live and then downstairs is the converted granny flat that my kids and I call home. Our flat isn't big, but it's cosy, and we love it.

Our home is in a beautiful leafy suburb just ten minutes north of Sydney, called Lane Cove. We're mad South Sydney Rabbitohs fans, my whole family that is, which also includes my brothers, Michael and Nick, sister-in-law Skye, and then Ally and Jonathan, my niece and nephew. We're a small but tight-knit family, and for the last seven months, we've been on a hell of a roller coaster ride. That's why, as it turned out, the ghosting by that company was actually a blessing in disguise.

I had been absolutely dreading taking Max to daycare. My birth injuries had been so severe that I found it extremely hard to bond with him for the first several months. Things were finally looking up, though. For the first time ever, Max wanted me and no one else. Not Mum or Rose, just me, his mumma.

Being ghosted by that company meant that, for the first time since she was in kindergarten, I had time to immerse myself in the start-of-school year activities with Rose. My baby girl had somehow grown into a young woman over the summer, just in time to start high school. Instead of working ridiculous hours and missing out on all of the morning teas, information afternoons, and suppers, I was going to be there for every single function, and I couldn't wait, much to Rose's amusement.

I was able to ignore the alert that came through on the school app a couple of weeks before the new school year started, telling parents that the time had come to purchase their children's bus passes. I realised as I read the message that Rose was no longer going to need one, at least for the time being. I was excited to realise that I was going to be able to drive my daughter to and from school. It had been such a hectic time since Max was born, and with the terrible time I'd had because of my injuries, that I hadn't been able to focus on Rose the way I always had in the past.

When the time did come at the end of January, spending twenty minutes every morning and afternoon reconnecting with my girl was exactly what our relationship needed. We talked, laughed, and even made up fictitious stories about some of the people we passed every day on our way to school. My mum thought we were a pair of weirdos, but she was enjoying her time hanging out with Max while I was gone too. She was finally starting to feel like herself again after her own horrible few months.

Mum has a condition called Menière's disease. If you've never heard of the condition, then I'm glad, because I wouldn't wish it on my worst enemy. It is absolutely gut-wrenching and heartbreaking to watch someone you love go through those attacks. It's hard to explain, but in simple terms, it's like a severe form of vertigo. The attacks usually involve severe ringing in the ear, dizziness, and vomiting. In my mum's experience, the attacks can last anywhere from a couple of hours to up to forty-eight hours.

Mum was first diagnosed with Meniere's disease about five years ago. She had been having the attacks for almost twelve months before they finally figured out what was happening. Watching my mother go through an attack was terrible. It made my brothers and I feel so hopeless and scared. She would have them every few days for months at a time, but then when she was diagnosed, I was able to give her injections that worked to lessen or often stop her symptoms altogether.

To everyone's relief, the attacks eventually became nothing more than an occasional moment of giddiness. We discovered that some people went into remission with their disease and it appeared that she was one of those lucky people. Mum didn't have an attack for almost four years, but then the stress of looking after me and my kids and worrying about my injuries plunged her back into her own fresh hell.

Back in October, as I was counting down to my operation, Mum had her most severe attack yet. It lasted for forty-eight hours, and nothing worked to stop the symptoms. She spent the next couple of weeks desperately taking her medications to no avail before I happened upon the name of a new medication. Thankfully, the new medication eased her symptoms, and eventually her Meniere's calmed back down.

Being ghosted by that company meant that I could help Mum now that she was finally getting better from those terrible attacks, and I was feeling better after my operation. It meant that she could enjoy her grandchildren and get back out into her beloved garden. It also meant that she was able to help me more with Max again, not only for me to be able to do those wonderful school runs with Rose but but also so that I could take time to tackle everything else I had on my plate.

I was excited to be able to take the time to start my podcast properly.

I had connected with a wonderful producer named Darren at one of Rose's end-of-school functions a few weeks earlier. He had been a radio producer and now ran his own podcast company. He loved the idea of what I was trying to do and agreed that my experience could be turned into something positive.

I was also excited to be able to bake up a storm for my dear friend Lindsay's baby shower. Lindsay and Chelsea were two of my best friends for over twenty years. The girls are two of four sisters, and I have often been confused as their sister as well. Their dad used to call me "number five" when he was still with us. Chelsea and Lindsay, like me, had gone through all sorts of heartache to have their own children and finding out that I wouldn't be working fifty-hour weeks in the lead-up to the big pink floral affair that Chelsea and I had started planning weeks earlier really excited me.

And of course, there was the impending post-operative follow-up appointment with my surgeon, Dr Anderson, or Jack, as I had finally started referring to him at his insistence. In the months when my birth injuries were becoming apparent, I truly felt like none of the doctors who treated me cared about what I was going through, but that all changed when I met Jack.

He was a kind, considerate, and genuine man who had a wife and three young sons. He truly understood the importance of empathy. From the moment I first walked into his office several months earlier, I felt like somebody was finally going to help me. Of course, the surgery was a lot more major and painful than what I ever could have imagined, but it wasn't because the serious nature of the operation wasn't explained properly. It was more a case of my tendency to downplay things. If there is such a thing as an anti-hypochondriac, then I guess you'd say

I was one. You may just say that never having been through anything quite as painful before, I simply didn't have anything to compare it to.

Either way, I was still as grateful as ever to Jack for fixing that terrible prolapse. I appreciated his candour about the reason for the prolapse as well. There was no doubt in Jack's mind that the combination of incorrect use of forceps in the delivery room and the carelessness by that same doctor, leaving large pieces of Max's placenta inside of me, were most certainly to blame.

I was both looking forward to and dreading my follow-up appointment. Of course, I was looking forward to being told that my surgery had been a success. For weeks afterwards, I was sure that the surgery hadn't worked, but by January I was starting to realise that perhaps, once again, my expectations were just not realistic. I was still having the issues with sitting, and I wasn't going to be running around in those three-inch heels any time soon, but I could tell that my body was getting there, slowly. I was starting to think that maybe the surgery had worked after all.

But one question still loomed. You see, my pregnancy with Max followed the successful transfer of one of my remaining two embryos. Those embryos that had been stored at my fertility clinic in Bondi for the longest time until my doctor, the most experienced specialist at the clinic and also the medical director, agreed to put me on something called an immune protocol.

After a number of miscarriages, it was discovered that my body was rejecting my pregnancies because of something called NK cells. The NK, or natural killer cells, were basically my body's immune response attacking what it saw as foreign bodies. Women with autoimmune issues, just like me, often had the problem. As it turned out, a couple of courses of antibiotics, steroids, and blood-thinning injections were just the recipe that we needed.

Eight-and-a-half months after my successful embryo transfer, I welcomed Max into the world. My plan had been to transfer my remaining embryo, to try for my third and last baby, once Max was about eight months old. But then the shit hit the fan. With my injuries came the news that I would no longer be capable of carrying another baby. The news was devastating the first time and equally so the second and third times, but in my mind, if I was able to heal completely, I would surely be able to go ahead with my plan to carry my last child.

By January, I had almost convinced myself that it was just a matter of time until I was going to be driving out to see my fertility specialist over in Bondi, ready to do it all over again. Almost. I think that hanging onto that shred of hope was one of the things that helped me get through my recovery. Deep, deep down, in a place that I tried to ignore, I knew that the possibility was slim. But I wasn't ready to give up on my dream of having my third and final baby.

Chapter 3
Mid-January 2023 Continued

My follow-up appointment was booked for mid-January, just days before Lindsay's baby shower. The weeks between school finishing and the day of my follow-up appointment passed too quickly. For the first time in months, I was able to spend time with my family without being in constant pain. For the first time since he was born, I could hold my son comfortably. Max had also finally started to enjoy spending time in his pram and in the car seat. We went for wonderful drives to the beach and the Blue Mountains. And one of our favourite things in the world to do was for Mum, the kids, and I to go for leisurely walks around the beautiful harbourside streets of Longueville, just minutes from home.

When the week of my appointment finally arrived, it was a busy one. I had the whole week booked up with baking and getting decorations made for the baby shower, with the exception of Tuesday morning when I headed off to see Jack for my follow-up. I left the house nice and early.

Jack had moved into a new room in the private suites of the same hospital where I'd had the operations to remove the retained placenta and repair the prolapse. I was surprised by the way I felt as I approached the front doors. I was so excited the last time I had walked in there, so ready to finally get myself better and move on with my life, but I'd been in so much pain when I walked out two days later.

Thinking back to that day, some nine weeks earlier, actually brought the threat of tears to my eyes. I had to do a quick mental check and remind myself that it was okay now. The trauma was still buried there, fairly close to the surface, which I hadn't realised until that moment.

The new rooms were pretty flashy compared to the tiny space that Jack and his secretary Helen had occupied previously. My appointment had been booked for 8:15 am, so when I walked in ten minutes early, I wasn't surprised to see that the waiting room was empty. By that point, I had met Jack half a dozen times in total. I truly appreciated the empathy he'd shown me and wished, as I had the first time I met him, that I had chosen him as my obstetrician from the start. I knew that he would have delivered my baby without destroying my body in the process, unlike the doctor who'd ended up delivering him. The doctor who turned up instead of the guy I'd actually been booked in with. But I was grateful that I'd found Jack to repair the terrible injuries I had sustained.

We chatted for several minutes about kids, holidays, and laptop colours before finally getting down to business. I had, until a few days earlier, still been bleeding on and off since my operation. I had panicked a couple of weeks earlier when the bleeding really ramped up, convincing myself that surely my stitches must have torn open. Thankfully, nothing of the sort had happened. Jack informed me that the bleeding was much more likely to be hormonal than anything else. My stitches were still intact, and I was told that if it happened again, there were medications I could try taking to settle things back down. I hadn't swum all summer, so it was good to know that I might just get a chance before the weather turned cold.

Once that was sorted out, there was only one question left to ask. Max was already seven months old, and I was eager to get moving on my plan for baby number three, or "stinker number two" as our next baby had affectionately been nicknamed by Rose. I tried a few times to explain that she too had once been a little smelly bum in a nappy but she wouldn't hear of it. As far as Rose was concerned, she'd walked herself off to the toilet within moments of being born. Of course, that wasn't how I remembered it, not by a long shot, but it was so sweet how adamant she was. The baby would be her "stinker number two" and that really did count as something special.

I took a deep breath before asking Jack nervously if anything had changed regarding carrying another baby. He knew that I had my last, perfect little 5AA graded embryo in storage, and he knew that I had been planning to try and have another child. He knew how much my plan meant to me, and that's why I knew what he was going to say before he even opened his mouth.

Jack looked sad. I saw the hesitation in his eyes as he looked down before speaking.

"I'm really sorry but nothing has changed there," he finally said.

"I thought that maybe there was still a small chance." I spoke slowly, trying not to sound too disappointed.

"It wouldn't be safe for you or the baby," He explained. "The weight of a baby would pull your uterus out of your body. It would be catastrophic for you both."

It was the same thing he'd told me several times before but it was the first time I had really heard him. I guess I had been in denial.

"I appreciate you being honest with me." I said. "I've started doing some research about surrogacy so at least now I can focus on what I need to do".

"You won't have any trouble finding someone to help you, Tabitha, I really believe that." He said it with such sincerity.

"I hope you're right!" I joked, as I wiped away my tears. Apologising as I did so. I hated people to see me cry, I always had.

"Please don't apologise." He said it with such kindness that I couldn't help but laugh, genuinely this time.

We talked for a few minutes about surrogacy when I realised something. I needed another guest for my podcast. I had recruited several women who wanted to discuss their own traumatic birth experiences and decided on five who I would feature in the first season of the podcast. Each of the women I'd spoken with was at a different stage of their journey, but they were all amazing and brave. Having Jack on my show to talk about things from a doctor's point of view was exciting. I couldn't believe I hadn't thought of it earlier.

As soon as I mentioned it, he agreed. I knew that he helped women overcome their birth injuries every day and that he would be a really valuable contributor. The thought of having the remarkable man who had repaired my broken pieces talking on the podcast was exciting.

I walked out to the reception once we were done, ready to pay my bill, but Jack reminded me that I didn't have anything to pay for our consultation. With that, I thanked both him and Helen again.

As I headed for the door, I made a mental note to send something to say thank you, maybe some wine and chocolates. Walking out of the front doors of the hospital not two minutes later, I felt hopeful. As I headed towards my car, I called Mum to check in. Rose and Max were finishing their breakfast, and Max was getting grumpy like he always did when he was due for a sleep. I assured her that I would be back soon to sort out my little stinker.

And then I remembered. Baby number three. I thought about all the research I'd done about surrogacy. I had been so sure that I would get the all-clear to carry that last baby myself, but it still hadn't stopped me from researching surrogacy just in case. As it turned out, I had read everything I could find on the subject. I just hoped that Jack was right about actually being able to find someone who would be willing to do something so remarkable for me.

Chapter 4
Late January 2023

I was eager to get started on my search for a surrogate straight away, but I knew I would have to put it on the back burner for a few days so that I could focus on the task at hand, Lindsay's baby shower. Lindsay and her husband Cam were so excited about the impending arrival of their little girl. Although they would have loved to have had five babies, they had decided that this baby was going to be their last. Big brothers Liam, almost six, and Harrison, who was turning three the week before the baby was scheduled to be born, were absolutely bursting with excitement about getting a baby sister. Liam, in particular, being a little bit older, and already an old hand at being a big brother, was counting down the days, despite the fact that she wasn't joining them for a few more weeks.

When Mum, my kids, nieces, and I arrived at Chelsea's house on the Saturday after my appointment, we were met by the excited big brothers-to-be who were blowing up pink and aqua-coloured balloons on the front porch with their cousins, Chelsea's kids. I unloaded dozens of cupcakes, brownies, and table decorations for the kids to carry into the house.

The moment we stepped inside, we were transported. The house had been transformed into a bunny wonderland. The pink and aqua theme we had agreed on was a girly nod to our love of the Rabbitohs. Chelsea, Cam, and I had spent the previous evening putting most of the streamers and cutouts up while they both got the food organised. Seeing everything in the light of day was fantastic, as was seeing Lindsay's face when she walked in a few minutes later with her mum and two youngest sisters.

The look of sheer joy on her face as she saw all the decorations and food was fantastic. She had originally insisted that she shouldn't have a baby shower, saying that it wasn't the done thing for a third baby. Chelsea and I had insisted that her baby girl should be celebrated, just like her boys had been, and so she agreed. Watching her take it all in warmed my heart. An hour later, the house was full of people who had come to celebrate my friend and her little girl.

We spent the afternoon eating, drinking, and playing games. We measured Lindsay's belly and unwrapped nappies to discover which variety of chocolate had been melted and smeared inside. It was beautiful to see how spoiled the mum and baby were, as well as the boys. Several people, including my family, had bought the boys gifts, which reminded me of my baby shower for Max. A few people had done the same thing for Rose, and I remembered with a smile how special it had made her feel. I could see the boys were just as thrilled.

The afternoon went far too quickly, as big events often do. By the time the last guests left, it was 5 pm. Somehow the kids were still hungry despite eating non-stop all afternoon, so Cam warmed up some of the mini pizzas he'd stashed in the fridge for them while Chelsea and I cleaned up. Mum and Lindsay tried to help at first but were quickly put in charge of feeding the kids instead. Cam, Chelsea, and I finished tidying the kitchen fairly quickly, and I was about to start pulling the decorations down in the lounge room when Lindsay called out from the dining room.

"Tabitha, what are you doing? Come here!"

"What's up? are you okay?" I asked, popping my head around the corner.

"Forget about the decorations, Cam can pull them down later, I've barely spoken to you all day!"

"There's Moscato here, my dear," Chelsea called out, waving half a bottle of wine in my direction.

"If I must! But just a small one." I smirked, grabbing the glass of wine from the bench before sitting between Mum and Lindsay at the dining table.

"I've been dying to know all day, have you found a surrogate yet? What do you have to do now that you need someone to carry the baby for you?" Lindsay asked without taking a breath.

It was lovely to see how excited my dear friend was about my plans now that I knew what I had to do to try and have my last baby. Both of the girls had been so supportive through the first months of Max's life. But it was only after my operation that I'd truly opened up about just how hard a time I'd had. I knew that they were going to be there to support me through the next part of my parenthood journey, just like Mum was. We had a little bit of time to kill before we had to get home, so I decided to tell them what I knew so far about surrogacy.

When I had first learned about the impact that my injuries would likely have on my ability to carry another baby, I'd immediately logged on to start doing some research about surrogacy. I had been so desperately hoping that somehow I wouldn't need to go ahead with the daunting process of finding a woman who would be willing to carry a child for me, but I didn't want to find myself in the position where I would have to start from scratch months down the track.

When I started Googling, I already knew the basics. I knew that there were two different types of surrogacy: altruistic surrogacy and commercial surrogacy. The former, altruistic surrogacy, was the only option in Australia if you were approved to start the process. For a woman, it was only possible if you had a medical condition that prevented you from being able to carry your own baby, or if you were a man, you could be approved to start the process if you were a single person wishing to become a parent or for gay couples who needed help bringing their baby into the world.

For a lot of hopeful, or intended parents, as we were called, there was the added complication of going through the IVF process so that there would be embryos to transfer into the surrogate's uterus. A lot of people seemed to call that process implantation, but the implantation part happens a few days later, when, or indeed if, the embryo succeeded in adhering to the walls of the uterus. The process of having embryos created in the first place was hardest for older women or men who often needed another woman to donate their eggs as well. In that respect, I was lucky. I already had my perfect little embryo frozen and waiting to grow into another beautiful, feisty little red-headed baby.

Once you were given the green light to go ahead and find a woman to carry your baby, the rules, because of the altruistic nature of surrogacy here in Australia, were extremely strict. From what I had read, it was illegal to pay the surrogate for anything outside of what could be considered as reasonable out-of-pocket expenses.

Things like medical expenses and medications, petrol, parking fees, time off work, and maternity clothes were the main things that would be considered reasonable expenses. The list of costs that you were allowed to cover was a lot easier to follow than the list of things you weren't.

Money was the first one. Of course, it was also the most obvious. The intended parent, or parents, were forbidden from offering money for anything outside the parameters of what was deemed a "reasonable expense." You couldn't offer cash, even to pay for something like a cleaner. An intended parent was forbidden from paying for a holiday or offering gifts of any monetary value, unless they were explicitly required for the surrogate so that she could carry the baby safely, such as prenatal vitamins or a fan if the last months of the pregnancy happened to fall during the summer months. The rules around altruistic surrogacy are extremely complicated, unlike the rules around commercial surrogacy.

Commercial surrogacy is where the intended parent, or indeed parents, enter into a business arrangement with a woman who will carry their baby for a sum of money. The fee, should the surrogate successfully carry the child to term, usually sits at around the $100,000 mark. Although it seemed, at least from what I'd read so far, that $120,000 (Aussie dollars, that is) wasn't an uncommon amount to pay for an experienced surrogate in a state like California.

The trouble with commercial surrogacy was that it was not, and still isn't, an option in Australia. If I wanted to go down that path, then I would have to do so through an agency in either America or certain European countries such as Greece or the Ukraine. Not only was commercial surrogacy big business in the US and Europe, but egg and sperm donation were as well. College students could pay off their student debts from a few donations. A single mother in some states could support her family for two years following the birth of the child they had carried.

At first, I was simply hopeful that it wouldn't cost anything like that to have my last baby, but by the time I was sitting in Lindsay's home, telling the women closest to me about my plans, I had discovered that the laws in New South Wales, the state where I lived, stated that it was actually illegal for me to even entertain the idea of overseas surrogacy anyway. The laws in Queensland and the ACT were the same. The reality was that I had no choice but to find a woman here in Australia.

Because the overseas option wasn't one that I was allowed to look into, I had made the decision that I was going to try and find someone close to me to help me. I had also joined an online group that I found on social media, a few months earlier, when I'd first started researching my options. A lot of intended parents, or IP's, posted ads in the group in the hope that they might meet a surrogate that way.

When I first joined the group, it was purely for research purposes for the podcast. I had asked a few questions about the process but I hadn't intended to do one of those ads myself. But then things changed when I saw Jack and finally had to face my new reality, that I could no longer carry the baby safely myself. The night after my appointment, I had decided to put myself out there and post my own introduction. I knew it was unlikely that I would connect with someone that way, but I figured that I had nothing to lose. There were women in the group who were looking for a family to help and I figured that I might as well throw my hat in the ring.

I had read that something like eighty per cent of intended parents found their surrogate within their existing networks. However, that still left the other twenty per cent who found someone via forums and groups just like the one I was in, so I decided that it was worth a try. It took me a few hours, but I finally posted my story with a picture of myself. I was honest about the fact that I already had two beautiful and healthy children but stopped short at adding their names or photographs, just in case.

The only people who had responded to the ad were several other IPs. They were, of course, looking for the same miracle that I was. Everyone was so kind and positive. Some of them had been searching for over a year with no success, which was a bit disheartening, but I tried not to let it get me down, remembering Jack's words again.

Most of the people who had replied to my post were still not parents at all, which made me feel guilty at first. I had two beautiful children to wrap my arms around. I got to spend every day with my own babies. I'd been living my best life as a mum for nearly thirteen years. I was luckier than so many people. I wondered if I should try to make peace with it and accept that my family was finished, but then I remembered my little embryo, my frosty, my future little stinky baby.

I had been through so much to get to where I was. I was finally feeling good—no, I was great. I would have my moments; often I'd sit down in a way that would remind me that I could no longer just throw myself down on the lounge. Or I'd cop a baby foot to the belly that reminded me of the tenderness that still lingered. But I had come so far. I was more in love with my kids every day. I loved being a mum again. Max was thriving; he was such a firecracker and a real little social butterfly. Rose was growing up so quickly and she was such a wonderful big sister. I wasn't ready to let go of my dream of bringing my last baby home.

The next step in my search for a surrogate wasn't yet completed. I explained to the girls that I was planning to ask a few of the women I knew as well but that I hadn't had time to figure out exactly who I was going to ask yet. Just as I was about to start explaining the process that I was planning to use so that I could narrow down my options, Max started to protest.

When I checked the time on my phone, I realised that I'd been talking and answering Mum and the girls' questions for nearly an hour. Even Cam had been fascinated and joined in the conversation. I knew that Max was tired because it was already past his bath time, and I knew that Lindsay's boys would be starting to get tired too. I noticed the three little boys on the lounge snuggled up with Rose while she read them a book and knew that my suspicions were correct: it was time to round everyone up and head home.

I told my friends that I would update them next time we spoke. By the time we next got together, I was sure that I would have something to add to the already complicated story. I was sure that I was going to figure out who to ask that night, once the kids were bathed and snuggled up in bed .

Chapter 5
February 2023

I sat down at my desk that night, once my big kid and my little one were snuggled up in their beds. It was a strange mixture of emotions that washed over me as I opened my laptop. I felt excited and terrified, full of hope and trepidation. I knew that what I needed to do next could make or break relationships with the women I intended to ask. I knew that I needed to approach that next task carefully. I was glad to have a plan.

I had spent the few days between my appointment and Lindsay's baby shower thinking about how I should approach my search for someone who might be willing and able to help me have my last baby. I had eventually decided that the best way would be to start with my Facebook page. I clicked into my friends list. And, oh, what an interesting exercise that was! After a quick scroll, I decided to use the same strategy that Rose had employed in the past whilst watching the show, *Millionaire Hot Seat*. I would use a process of elimination.

Of the roughly 500 Facebook friends I had, I first eliminated the men. This may not be the most politically correct admission to make in this day and age, but I was pretty sure that my brothers, Nick, Michael, and my friend Theo, among others, would probably think I had finally lost my marbles altogether if I'd asked for their help.

Next, it was my English and American friends. As I deleted their names from the spreadsheet where I had pasted everyone's names, I realised that I had a couple of beautiful women, half a world away, who would probably have raised their hands to help me in an instant, had it been at all possible.

After completing the first two steps of the elimination process, I was left with 126 people. I pondered for quite a while what the next step should be before messaging Mum for her opinion. Understandingly, at least in hindsight, Mum wasn't much help. Surrogacy was almost unheard of in her day; she'd had her own children in her early to mid-twenties. If Mum had had a nice husband, a supportive and gentle-natured partner, I believe she would have ended up with her own reality show—she would have had ten babies, at least! She loved being a mum more than anything in the world—well, until she'd had grand babies—but she told me that she couldn't possibly influence such a huge decision. I understood, so I stepped back at that point. I needed some time to ponder my next move.

I spent an hour writing questions for my upcoming interview with Dr. Jack for my podcast before hopping into bed that night. I went to sleep thinking about how I was going to further narrow down that list and figure out who I could ask to carry my baby and indeed how I could do so.

✧ ✧ ✧

It was three days later, while Max ate his lunch, that I finally got the chance to grab my laptop and continue with the task at hand. I was ready to continue the search within my own circle of friends and family for my surrogate. It was such a glorious summer day that I decided to join Mum, Max, and Teddy the cat on the back patio.

I had decided over the previous few days that the most sensible next step would be to eliminate women who either hadn't finished their families or were past the age where they would be able to safely have another baby. That step more than halved the number of women, leaving me with just thirty-seven. I pondered the names staring back at me from my computer screen. One by one, I considered what my relationship was with the women. I was going to be asking for someone to make a huge sacrifice for me; I knew that I couldn't approach it lightly.

Almost an hour after sitting down at my desk, I had narrowed my list down to four women. Josephine was a good friend that I'd met almost twenty years earlier at work. We'd become closer since having our kids, and I didn't think that she had had any issues during her pregnancies. Josephine was a few years younger than me at forty-one. My fertility specialist in Bondi, who I'd talked to about my plans, had suggested I find someone under the age of forty to carry my baby. The younger the woman was, the less complications she was likely to experience during the pregnancy.

Then there were two of my cousins, who were actually sisters. I knew that they had both finished their families and that they too had both enjoyed being pregnant. The oldest of the girls, Kaitlin, had three children, the youngest of whom was almost four. Whilst the younger of the two sisters, Carrie, had adorable twins, a girl and a boy. The twins were five and had recently started kindergarten. My cousins were a lot younger than me, Kaitlin was thirty-eight and Carrie was thirty-two, so they were both well within the age range that my doctor had suggested would be optimal.

The last woman on my list was my sister-in-law Skye. Skye and Nick had been together for about twenty-three years. She was actually in Year 12 when they'd met. Nick had been twenty-two and his son Jonathan had been just two years old. I know I would have run a mile at that age if I'd met a guy who had a child, but they had been a perfect match. I'd never met such a well-matched couple. Over the years, our families had become close. I often referred to her parents and younger sister as my in-laws; it made it easier to explain how they fit into my family.

Narrowing my search down to those four women was exciting and terrifying, but it was just the beginning. The next step was going to be a lot harder. I would need to sit down and write a detailed letter to each of the women, asking if they would do me the honour of becoming my surrogate. I would be asking them about carrying my baby and bringing them safely into the world before handing him or her over for me to raise.

Of course, I wouldn't be sending the emails all at once. It wasn't one of my well-crafted marketing emails; it wasn't going to be a case of hit and hope. I couldn't just hit send and hope that a percentage of my target audience would respond favourably. The next step from there was deciding which woman I was going to approach first, second, and so on.

By the time I had finalised my list, Max was starting to protest. He had finished his lunch and had become bored of mushing his leftover Vegemite scroll in his hair. He had had a wonderful time laughing at Teddy the cat whilst Mum had been feeding him, but he'd had enough. My sweet baby had started saying "mum-mum" a few weeks earlier, and he'd quickly learned how to use my name to convey his thoughts and wishes. It was adorable, even when he was using it in that tired and cranky voice.

So I closed my computer, popped it back inside on my desk, and then took Max inside to get him down for his afternoon nap. Once he was asleep, I started the next part of the daunting task: writing the letters. I often wonder how on earth we ever got by without smartphones. As little Max slept soundly on my lap, I wrote the draft copies of those four letters. The only thing left was to try and figure out who I was going to ask first.

Chapter 6
Early March 2023

After going back and forth for a few days, I finally decided that I would ask my older cousin Kaitlin first. Although she was older than her sister, it had played on my mind that the younger of the two, Carrie, only had the twins, and so, although she had recently told me that she had finished having babies, her children were only young and so was she.

Carrie had split with the twins' father a couple of years earlier, and I knew that she would never consider having another baby on her own, but she loved babies and she still had plenty of time to meet someone else and have more children.

Kaitlin, on the other hand, had only intended to have two children. The youngest had been an unexpected surprise—an absolute blessing, but definitely the last baby. The family had recently moved up to the Gold Coast, so logistically it might be a little complicated, but I knew that she was going to be coming back to Sydney for conferences and seminars. Plus, if she agreed to help me, she could do all of her appointments and scans near home. The clinic where my little frosty baby was stored had sister clinics in every capital city. The process of the embryo transfer only took a matter of minutes. I could fly her down, take her for a quick trip to see my doctor, followed by a spot of lunch, and have her back home before anyone even realised she was gone.

What a crazy thought it was. I'd actually realised, after overthinking things for the umpteenth time, that I needed to hit send on the email that I had written so carefully before I lost my nerve completely, and so I did. I spent the next several minutes refreshing my email. Our wifi was shoddy at best—it was ridiculous. We lived so close to the Sydney CBD, less than ten minutes, yet our internet was terrible. The mobile reception in the whole area was rubbish too. I didn't want to miss her response, if or when she emailed me back.

But the days passed without a word. I'd gone back and checked the email address, just to be sure that it was correct. It was. I felt sick. Maybe I should have put a read receipt on the email, if that was even a function on my Hotmail account. I realised that it had never occurred to me at the time when I'd sent the email. How dumb could I be?

I had no way of knowing if the email had been read. Had my cousin been so busy between three kids, two jobs, and a husband that she hadn't even read the email? Maybe she'd read it and was considering it, or maybe she'd seen it and felt uncomfortable or angry. I felt like a teenager who'd finally built up the courage to ask out their crush, only to hear crickets. It wasn't a nice feeling. Actually, it was pure torture.

By the time two weeks had passed, I had tried, unsuccessfully, to recall the email. I was completely gutted. I had put my heart and soul into that email. There were several outs; I'd written my letters based on the suggestions of people in the online surrogacy group. They were people who had successfully found a surrogate and held that precious woman's hand as she'd given birth to their baby. One of the constant themes when it came to writing your letter, or letters, was to give the woman the opportunity to say no. To ensure that they could feel comfortable enough to tell you that although they were flattered, and honoured, they could not, for whatever reason, go on the journey with you.

I was in limbo. I wasn't sure what to do. I realised that asking the younger sister was no longer an option and so I filed her email away in the IVF folder that I'd created over ten years earlier. I felt so hopeless, until I noticed the invoice for the transfer that had resulted in my beautiful little boy. I couldn't believe that his first birthday was fast approaching, that it had been almost a year since I'd walked into the hospital with a silly pumpkin t-shirt covering my huge belly. The belly with the little wriggly boy nestled inside. Max was an absolute miracle; I had to believe that everything would work out for the best one more time.

Finding that invoice helped me put things into perspective. I was sad that my cousin hadn't felt that she could talk to me or even email me back. I had to believe that she had a good reason. I knew that she'd had some challenges in recent times; she'd left Sydney and moved a thousand kilometres away from her friends and most of her family. That couldn't have been an easy thing to do. I made peace with the way things had turned out. I had to, for my own sanity and for the sake of our relationship.

It was going to be awkward as hell the next time we ended up in a room together. I'd be drawing on the course I had attended several years earlier about having difficult conversations, big time. I knew that I would have to get over it, if not for my own sake then at least for Mum's sake, but I wasn't sure how I could possibly ask someone else. The feeling of rejection wasn't something I wanted to subject myself to again, but I knew that I was going to have to risk it or give up on my dream. I reminded myself that I was not a quitter. After everything I had overcome after Max's birth, I knew that I would dust myself off and try again.

Chapter 7
21ˢᵗ March 2023

I had been fairly active on social media since giving birth to Max. I had been absolutely overwhelmed by the support I'd received after I'd posted anonymously about my mum's Meniere's attacks. The community of women had been so kind, at a moment when I had needed it more than ever. I'd been able to get Mum a new remedy for her illness, and although it hadn't put her completely back into remission, it had certainly helped.

Since embarking on the journey to find a surrogate, I had become even more active. I had found the community of kind, generous, and wonderful people who were either looking to find, or indeed become, a surrogate. There were also many people who had already embarked on the journey in one capacity or another.

There were individual groups for hopeful intended parents and potential surrogates. I always kept up to date with the IP group, but most of my time was spent in the mixed group. The group was private, which was done in order to protect our privacy. When I realised that my cousin wasn't going to respond to my email, it was members of that main group who really helped me to overcome the feelings of regret and rejection. The people, mostly women, in the group were so understanding and encouraging. They made me understand that my feelings were normal and completely valid and really helped me move on from the failed attempt at asking for help.

I had made a few friends from the group by that point too, one of whom lived in Gladesville, a suburb just fifteen minutes from Lane Cove. She too was a single mum and had also sustained terrible injuries during her child's birth. Her name was Lara and she was hoping to find a surrogate who would be willing to have two embryos transferred at once.

We had met for coffee with the babies. Her little girl was about six months older than Max. It had been a wonderful experience because, although the few people close to me who knew about that last baby I was trying to have were so very supportive, none of them truly understood.

I got the impression that Mum, Chelsea, and Lindsay were worried. The whole thing was such a strange concept for most people. I understood their concerns, especially around the legal implications of having another woman carry my baby. The woman would legally be the baby's mother at the birth, regardless of whose DNA the child carried. The IP, in this instance me, would have to go through the process of legally adopting the child—my child. And so it was amazing to find a friend who was on the same journey to have her last baby, or babies in Lara's case, as I was.

Social media was a lifeline for so many different people with different stories and needs. My possible lifeline was sitting in my Facebook "others" folder. As it turned out, it had been sitting there for over a week.

I'm sure I'm not the only one who never checks their social media "others" folder. Whenever I did, I usually found myself visually assaulted by unwanted photos of both men and women who had clearly never been told about the future ramifications of sending nudes out into the world wide web. Then there were the Indian princes and billionaires who were looking for an Australian princess to marry. As flattering as their offers were, I'd always been more of a Russell Crowe, Chris Hemsworth, and Channing Tatum girl. I couldn't help it; I just preferred my men with pretty eyes and muscles.

So Imagine my surprise when a lady I hadn't spoken with before responded to my introduction post in the surrogacy group. Her name was Tania and she had written a comment on my post, asking if I had seen her private message. What was she talking about? I definitely had not seen a message from her. I responded immediately. Was she sure I was the one she'd meant that comment for? I hadn't seen anything.

Immediately I checked my messages, and sure enough, below my most recent marriage proposal, there was a message from Tania. It had been dated the 27th of February, just over a week earlier. The message had come through just a few days after I'd sent the email to my cousin.

Tania's message was brief, a quick introduction followed by her reason for messaging me. As it turned out, she had seen me interacting in the group since I'd joined a few months earlier and had been impressed by my story, the courage I'd shown through my injuries, and my determination to finish my family despite no longer being able to carry another baby. I hadn't even told the full story. If I was going to find a surrogate, I didn't want them to help because they felt sorry for me, but at the same time I had wanted to be transparent about why I had ended up in the group, looking for someone to carry my precious baby.

I wasted no time in responding to both the message and the comment that Tania had left on my post. I immediately apologised, explaining that I hadn't seen her message and that it had been a crazy week. I'd written something about the nudes and princes being to blame but then thought twice about sending that part. This was serious, and I didn't want to mess things up with a stupid joke. I asked if she would like to talk on the phone sometime, or, assuming she didn't live too far away, would she like to grab a coffee?

Half an hour later, I heard the sound of my messenger pinging with a message on my phone. Max was chewing on the last of his lunch, so I checked my messages, and sure enough, it was once again Tania saying that she would love to have a coffee. We lived a matter of minutes away from each other, as it turned out, and she was off work with her two- and three-year-olds for her maternity leave. She had mentioned in her first message that she was taking another year or so off.

It occurred to me that a year was plenty of time to have a baby and be healed in time to get back to work. My thoughts were interrupted by the sound of my phone again; this time it was an apology. One of the girls had had a run-in with her bookshelf and needed ice cream to fix it. I smiled, thinking about the number of times Rose had been fixed up with treats at a similar age. We quickly agreed on a time to meet for coffee the following week before signing off.

We agreed to leave our babies with their nannas for our first meeting. We wanted to meet without the stress of tired babies and toddlers. I'd have been happy to see her with a marching band performing whilst the kids did somersaults at the table, but just the two of us worked well too.

When the day finally arrived, I made sure I was at my favourite cafe, Garçon, a few minutes early. I felt like I was waiting for a blind date. It hadn't occurred to me, for even a second, to ask Tania what she would be wearing. To say it was an awkward wait was a definite understatement. Of course, I'd had a look at her social media page, as I'm sure she had mine, but like mine, her profile was locked.

The new trend of replacing pictures with avatars meant that there was no actual photo that I could see. I understood her need to maintain her privacy. I'd seen some wonderful stories about people who had successfully found a surrogate and gone on to have their babies, but there were also some heartbreaking stories of both IPs and surrogates who had been scammed.

There were stories of surrogates who had become pregnant, only to have their IPs, people they'd built a trusting relationship with—or so they thought—refuse to pay legitimate medical bills. One woman had even had her IPs, a couple who'd been trying for five years to have a baby, go back on their promise to pay for her to take six weeks off work after she'd had a scheduled caesarean to deliver their baby. I'd seen stories of women who would get their IPs' hopes up, insisting that they wanted to help, only to ghost them. I understood Tania's need to maintain her privacy at this point, just as I was conscious about protecting myself and my family.

I needn't have worried though. I recognised Tania the moment she walked into the little French cafe in Lane Cove. She was tall and slim, with green eyes and long brown hair with blonde highlights and actually looked like her avatar, right down to the white cropped t-shirt and denim skirt. She was stunning. Unlike my experience with online dating, this woman was exactly the same in person as what she had been during our initial conversations. My nerves completely dissipated the moment that Tania wrapped her arms around me.

"Hi gorgeous!" She squealed as soon as she saw me, wrapping her arms around me.

"Oh wow, hi." I said, smiling, immediately being swept up in her excitement.

"You look like the cartoon thing on your Facebook profile." She said as she looked down at my boots. "Right down to those."

I couldn't help but laugh. Her presence was just so calming. She instantly felt like a familiar old friend. I wasn't at all surprised that the next hour and a half went far too quickly.

We talked about our families, parenting girls, and now, for me, the differences I was noticing as I learned how to parent a little boy. We also talked about how we had each found ourselves in the surrogacy group to begin with. Tania told me that she had always planned to help another family have a baby once she had finished having her own children, and I was truly touched by her reason.

Tania came from a large Italian family; she was the youngest of six kids. The oldest of her siblings, Marcus, was twelve years her senior and he was gay. Marcus and his husband Patrick had met at university and become serious fairly quickly, both agreeing that they wanted to start a family before they were twenty-five. The reality of Marcus and Patrick having children was not as easy as they had assumed it would be, though.

Tania explained that the process of finding an egg donor was relatively simple. They had a number of lesbian friends, one of whom was a woman who had no interest in having children of her own. Their friend was happy to do two back-to-back egg donor cycles to give her friends as many chances of becoming parents as she could. The cycles worked and Marcus and Patrick had nine embryos cryogenically frozen while they started their search for a surrogate.

Tania was just thirteen when her brother and Patrick were on that roller coaster, the same age as my own daughter. She remembered coming home from school one day to see her big brother crying to their mum because, after another false start, he was worried that they would never find a woman who would be willing to carry their baby for them.

A few months later, they finally found a woman who was willing to help, and a year or so after that they welcomed their twins but Tania never forgot the heartbreak of seeing her big brother crying to their mother. That day was cemented in her mind and in her heart. She made the decision all those years ago that, once she was finished having her own children, she would carry a baby for someone who was unable to do so.

Tania's intention had always been to carry a baby for a gay couple, but then she saw my story. My new friend seemed genuinely touched by my story, and I was thankful when she then brushed off my concern about my age. I had worried that at forty-six, my age could be a huge deterrent for someone who would otherwise be interested in helping me, but I needn't have worried. Tania assured me that age was not going to be a factor, even suggesting that, had she not known any better, she would have put me closer to my late thirties. I was flattered beyond words.

When the time came to get back to our babies, I insisted on paying the bill. At first, Tania refused, but it was the least I could do. Tania had left her girls at home with her mum so that she could come and meet me. She was thinking about carrying my baby, bringing stinker number two into the world for me, so I told her that I wasn't taking no for an answer. The least I could do was buy her a piece of cake and a coffee.

As we walked outside, I began to feel nervous again. I wasn't sure what to say, but within a moment, Tania squeezed me tight in another one of her big bear hugs.

"I'm so glad we met." She told me, with the same infectious smile that she'd worn for the whole coffee date.

"Thank you so much for coming, you're a sweetheart," I said, feeling once again at ease.

"Let me give you a buzz after I talk to hubs, ok?" She said as she hugged me again.

"Ok, thank you, lovely." And with that she turned and headed towards the lifts.

And then Tania was gone. I stood for a moment, not quite sure if I was imagining the last ninety minutes. Had Tania really mentioned next steps? If I didn't know better, I would think that I had just met my surrogate. The gorgeous and kind woman with her larger-than-life personality and smile to match was seriously considering giving my family the ultimate gift. I could not have felt better if I'd won the lottery. With a spring in my step, I headed over to the sushi place at the other end of the plaza to grab Rose a treat for dinner before heading home.

Chapter 8
Late March 2023

I hadn't expected to hear from Tania so soon after our catch-up, but that evening, at exactly 9:43 pm, I received a text. We had swapped phone numbers earlier and agreed to communicate that way going forward. Tania had spoken with her husband Brendan. They both agreed that they would like to have a family picnic so that we could all meet each other. I was eager to organise our next get-together as soon as possible.

Rose didn't have any weekend sport in term one of school, so we agreed to meet for an early dinner a few days later on Saturday. I invited Mum, but she didn't want to impose. She was happy to let me make this decision about my little family and assured me that she would meet everyone for the next catch-up, all going well.

The rest of the week dragged on. Finally, after what felt like a hundred days, it was time to meet Tania's little family and to introduce her to mine. Rose, Max, and I arrived at the national park just before 3 pm, about ten minutes early, in case there was an issue with parking. Thankfully, we found a parking spot just metres away from where we'd agreed to meet. Rose and I unloaded the picnic blanket, food, and baby bags from the car and then loaded Max into his pram. We headed over to an empty picnic table that was sheltered from the afternoon sun.

The tables were so popular that people often arrived to reserve them for birthday parties at 7 am. There were streamers and food in the bin right near the table. We must have been lucky because clearly there had been a party there not long ago. I took it as a good sign.

Rose and I had just started setting the food out on the table when I heard that already familiar voice.

"Hi!" Shouted Tania.

I looked up to see her waving excitedly as she pushed a huge double pram towards us. There was a tall, friendly looking guy with olive skin and short, dark hair walking beside her. I assumed it was Brendan. He had a cooler bag and picnic blanket on one arm, a nappy bag over the other shoulder and a beer in his hand.

I waved as they approached.

"Tabitha, this is Brendan." She announced, gesturing towards her husband.

I stuck my hand out, expecting him to shake it but instead he wrapped his arms around my shoulders. I laughed as I realised that he was a hugger too.

"And these are the monkeys, Isabella and Ava."

"Hi girls, how are you?" I asked, I could see that the girls attention was focussed on Rose and Max. "This is Rose and baby Max."

Isabella and Ava were the spitting image of their mum, minus the blonde highlights. The girls were fascinated by Rose and Max. They were a little bit shy at first, but I wasn't surprised that Rose had them chatting away excitedly in no time. They hadn't met a big girl like Rose before apparently but they were quite the authority on baby boys, since their auntie had a big one in her tummy. Once the introductions were all done, we walked together back to the picnic table. We chatted easily about the weather and kids while we set out all the food.

Max was fascinated by his new friends and seemed to be enjoying the extra attention as they all sat down on the picnic blanket, ready for dinner.

When the girls all had their plates of food, it was time to sit Max in his pram to feed him. Once he was strapped in and munching on a dinosaur nugget it was time to talk about why we were all there. I wasn't sure how to broach the subject but before I had a chance to get stressed out about it, Brendan spoke.

"I hope you don't mind that Tania told me about your injuries." He said "I can't believe how much you had to fight for the doctors to take you seriously."

"It was ridiculous. For months they really made me feel like I was imagining things."

"I've been doing research about birth injuries and it's unbelievable how many women deal with such terrible injuries," Tania said. "I'm so glad you and other women are speaking out."

"It's been a crazy time. things have changed so much, and even more so now that I can't have another one of these." I smiled, a little sadly, as I stroked Max's hair.

"You're a lovely mum babe". Tania remarked, as she reached out and squeezed my hand. "I know you mentioned that you're open to becoming an extended family with your surrogate. If we end up going ahead that would be important to Brendan and me."

"Absolutely!" I exclaimed. "I would want that too. Family to me is so much more than just blood." I explained my relationship with Chelsea, Lindsay and their family as an example.

"That's great, it definitely would impact our decision to go ahead with things." Brendan added.

I nodded, smiling, as Max started squealing at the sight of his strawberries. I wondered if my next baby would love fruit and hate vegetables the way Max did, and whether they would be calm like Rose, or a crackerjack like their brother.

I looked over at Rose, Isabella and Ava on the picnic blanket. The girls were eating their dinner and chatting about Peppa Pig, ballerinas and high school. The little girls were fascinated by Rose's long golden hair. The little girls told my daughter that she looked like Rapunzel. Rose was thrilled since Rapanzel had apparently overtaken Ariel as her favourite princess. I loved the natural affinity that my daughter had with other kids, especially little ones. She had always been that way and it never ceased to make me swell with pride.

Max was fascinated with Brendan and Tania, especially Brendan. My boy was constantly surrounded by women, but when my brothers, nephew, Cam, and other men were around, he seemed to understand that he was one of them. I could imagine him running around with the guys playing footy soon enough, and I loved it. It had been so hard during those early months when I was in so much pain. Max truly hated leaving the house back then, and I had despaired that we would be stuck at home forever. Seeing how much of a social butterfly he had become really warmed my heart.

The way Max responded to Tania and Brendan told me more than anything else could have. I had always believed that small children and animals knew when people were good or bad. They hadn't been conditioned by society to accept bad behaviour as normal. They had a sixth sense that warned them when someone couldn't be trusted, but it was clear that Max sensed that our friends were good people, and I believed him. Because I felt it too. I could only hope that they felt the same way about me. I guess I'd find out soon enough.

Before I knew it, a week had passed since the picnic. We had hesitantly packed up and headed back to our cars a little after 6:30 pm. The time had flown by once again. The kids all had a wonderful time as well. Max had won over Isabella and Ava once he'd joined them back on the picnic blanket after dinner. Rose had popped a few toys in his nappy bag, including the sweet giraffe teething toy that she had given him for Christmas. The girls were absolutely smitten with their new friends and they made Rose promise that she would pick them up from daycare one day so that she could meet their friends. She didn't have the heart to tell them that she was too young to drive and instead she nodded along excitedly.

I felt like I'd made new friends for life. Of course, I was so hopeful that they would make the decision that Tania would become my surrogate, but if not, I really hoped that we could still be friends. I completely understood and agreed when she messaged that night, once the girls were in bed, to let me know that she was going to take a week to make her decision. The whole family loved us. They'd gotten a great vibe from us. She said that it was clear that we weren't fake and that there was a lot of love in our little family. The admission had brought tears to my eyes. I had felt the same way about them. I could see them becoming part of our already unconventional but happy little family. I was full of so much love and hope for the future as I headed back in to bed that night .

I could not believe how quickly the year was already going. We spent Good Friday at the Sydney Royal Easter Show. We hadn't been able to enjoy the show properly for a few years thanks to Covid, so we spent an enjoyable but exhausting day walking through all of the pavilions, looking at farm animals, decorated cakes, and huge artworks made completely out of Australian produce. We ate huge Dagwood dogs, pizza, and chips on a stick followed by ice creams. And my favourite part of the day, just as it had been since I was a little girl, the showbags. Max had never seen so many weird and wonderful things before, so I wasn't at all surprised when he fell asleep almost immediately that night.

The next day, we had our annual Easter Saturday lunch with Lindsay, Cam, Chelsea, and the kids. Rose and Max had met little Eleanor a couple of times by then, and they were both smitten, especially Rose, who'd been allowed to have a cuddle. Max adored the baby from a little further away since he'd developed a love of whacking things. Harrison had given Max a spade that they'd been playing with at Balmoral Beach a couple of weeks earlier, and he loved playing his baby piano with it. I didn't want to risk him practicing his new skill on my friend's daughter.

It always made me smile watching the kids interact with each other. Chelsea's son Josh was only six months younger than Rose, and then her daughter Milly was eighteen years old. Even though there were some pretty big age gaps mixed into the group, they were always the best of friends whenever they saw each other.

The food and drink flowed as easily as the conversation. We talked about Chelsea's upcoming holiday with the kids and mine. We both happened to be heading up to the Gold Coast in the first week of the holidays, so we'd planned to do a theme park day together. We talked about Lindsay and Cam's renovation plans, which sounded amazing, and then , the news that everyone had been waiting for. I'd already talked my friends through every meetup and conversation with Tania, but they were dying to know whether I'd received an answer yet. But I hadn't.

I had spoken with Tania briefly a few times since our little family picnic the weekend before but we hadn't talked about the surrogacy plans again. The plan had been for her and Brendan to take the week before they made their decision. I had assured her at the time that they should take all the time they needed but she had assured me that a week would be plenty of time.

I wasn't expecting to hear from her until that evening, so I had tried not to check my phone constantly. I needn't have worried; there was nothing I couldn't tell Lindsay and Chelsea. They had been like sisters for a large chunk of my life.

They knew what I'd been through to have my little boy. It had been Lindsay who had encouraged me to keep going after my last couple of miscarriages. When I thought my heart couldn't possibly take any more, they had been the first ones I'd told, after Mum and Rose, about the tiny little life growing inside of me.

They'd been there for me on the terrifying night early in my pregnancy as I'd sat in the hospital waiting room, convinced that I was losing my baby. They had both had their own devastating losses. And now, they knew how desperately I wanted one more baby so they didn't think anything of me picking up my phone every few minutes. I'd thought to myself as we chatted effortlessly, reminiscing about so many adventures, and a few misadventures that we'd shared over the years just how lucky I was to have those women in my life.

Eventually, Max and Harrison started to get grumbly, despite Max having almost an hour-long nap in his pram. We were in the habit of taking our cues from the little kids, and so with that, we had started tidying up and getting ready for my kids and I to take our leave.

By the time we'd kissed and hugged everyone at least thirty times, and the boys had excitedly shown Rose their new Rabbitohs pyjamas and blankets, it was 4:03 pm. Fifteen minutes later, we were on our way. As I drove home, I realised that spending the day with my friends and our kids had been a great distraction from the impending conversation with Tania. I was only hours from learning about whether my new friend was going to help me have my baby.

I took the motorway home from Lindsay's place. It probably only saved ten minutes, but I was keen to get the kids fed and bathed before the Easter bunny came that night. Max was exhausted from his busy day and was once again asleep within ten minutes of lying down. It normally took an hour at least before I could put my little sweet boy in his cot. I was thankful, though, as I had so much to do for our Easter lunch the following day.

I spent some time tidying the kitchen bench before moving onto the toys that Max had thrown out of his playpen; the last thing we wanted was for the Easter bunny to break his neck in the middle of the night.

8 pm came and went, and I still hadn't heard from Tania. I had to stop myself a couple of times from spiralling. I reminded myself that even if she wasn't able to help me have my baby, she certainly thought that I was worthy of helping and that was huge. I tried to be a good, kind, and generous person; that's not to say I was perfect, not by a long shot.

I sometimes raised my voice and I could definitely be kinder to people who didn't say thank you when I let them in whilst driving. I was guilty of dropping F-bombs in front of my kids more than once, but I tried. Every day I tried to be the best version of myself. If I stuffed up, I would apologise and I would try not to make the same mistakes again, especially if my actions hurt others.

I had to believe that the good in me counted for something. With that thought in mind, I ushered Rose off to clean her teeth and get ready for bed. She tried to argue that it was far too early, but a quick reminder about the Easter bunny and she was in the bathroom in a flash.

By the time I got into bed half an hour later, I was exhausted. Max was still sound asleep, exhausted from the socialising earlier in the day. I didn't want to go to sleep yet in case I missed a message from Tania, so I pulled up the to-do list on my phone. We were heading off to Queensland in just over two weeks. I had booked our flights and car hire weeks earlier, but I still hadn't got around to doing a packing list. I tended to overpack for trips, just as I had initially done with my hospital bag when I was getting ready to go and have Max. The car we had hired would only have room for two large suitcases and a few smaller bags. Mum and I were heading away with my kids and my nieces, Brittany and Ally, so between the six of us, I needed to really plan down to the wire.

I had finished my list and was halfway through Rose's when I got an SMS from Tania. I was terrified that I was just about to have my heart broken, but I couldn't leave it until the morning. I immediately clicked on the message..

She started off by apologising for sending the message so late. They'd had friends over and it had been such a lovely day that the kids had stayed in the pool until almost six. They had ended up ordering pizza for dinner and had finally just gotten the girls down to bed.

The next paragraph was, like the message from a week earlier, a beautiful message about how her family had felt so comfortable around my children and me. She said again that she and Brendan could see how much I adored my children and that my love for them really showed in their happy natures. I was once again flattered. We're often our own critics. I'd been pretty hard on myself through those tough months following Max's birth. So to see myself through that woman's eyes, I remembered how far I'd come from those weeks and months.

As I read Tania's message, I couldn't believe the words in front of me. I was going to have my last little stinker. I had found my surrogate .

I had to hold my hand over my mouth whilst I got up out of bed. I managed to sit on the lounge before the strangest sound escaped my lungs. It was somewhere between a scream, a laugh, and a sob. I tried to read the message again, but I couldn't see clearly through my tears. I realised that I would need to write back.

Since Mum had made me turn on read notifications on my phone, I didn't want Tania to think I'd seen her message and just ignored it. I managed to find a huge thank-you gif to send. I replied then to say that I was honoured. I said I would touch base on Monday to talk about what needed to happen next. Once I'd calmed down, I quietly hopped back into bed. I kissed my babies a million times, and eventually, almost an hour later, I fell into a deep, dreamless sleep.

Chapter 9
April 2023

As I opened my eyes, the first thing I noticed was a toy bunny I'd never seen before, sitting in Max's cot. The sun was just starting to come up, and I saw the blue foil-covered egg in front of the bunny. It was Max's first Easter, and I couldn't wait until he and Rose woke up so that we could go and see what else the Easter bunny had left. Then I remembered. Instantly my eyes welled up again, but I was determined to keep the news to myself, for the time being at least.

There would be a number of tests run to make sure that Tania was able to carry another baby. There would be blood tests, scans, and several counselling sessions. I'd need to kick-start things ASAP. From speaking with my fertility specialist and people in my online group, I knew that the whole process usually took two to three months. I'd already done the calculations: all going well, I could have my last precious baby in my arms by Easter the following year.

I had to somehow get all of the appointments organised and attended if Tania wanted me there, whilst also being completely present for my babies. I needed to enjoy every moment with them before the madness of having a newborn in the house started all over again. I felt a pang of guilt, or maybe it was regret, at that moment. I wasn't sure what it would do to my bond with Max, having another baby that would need to be cuddled and loved. Would he resent the baby for taking his mum? At least by then he'd be walking. I wouldn't be in pain and trying to heal from all sorts of injuries and infections like I had been when he was a newborn. I certainly had enough love to give another baby, and I was sure my kids would too.

My thoughts were interrupted by Max rolling onto his tummy and giving me his morning smile. Max woke up at about 11 pm every night like clockwork. He was well past his nighttime bottles, but I'd discovered pretty quickly that he was waking for cuddles, so he would find himself in bed with me for the rest of the night. Every day when my baby boy woke up, he would stare at my face until he caught my attention. Sometimes I would be on my phone, checking my email or my socials, other times I would still be asleep until I sensed the movements next to me. In both scenarios, I would look over to catch his eye and be rewarded with the biggest smile. It was a pretty great way to start the day.

It was a matter of minutes later that Rose suddenly sat bolt upright in bed. It always amused me. On Christmas, Easter, and her birthday, every year from the time she was only little, Rose would do the same thing. One minute she'd be fast asleep, the next she'd be wide awake and sitting up in bed, in a panic to explore the house for untold treasures. Even at almost thirteen, she was still doing it. I loved it, and a big part of me hoped that she would never grow out of it.

Normally, I would leave the kids in my bed to play with plush toys whilst I had a quick shower and made Max's morning bottle, but Rose was so eager to find what goodies had been left around the house that I told her to go and have a quick look then come back. But she didn't want to see anything without me, so off we went, as the sun rose on that perfect Easter morning, to see what the Easter bunny had left.

Max had never tried chocolate before. He had no understanding of what all the shiny things all over the floor were, but Rose's excitement was infectious. Each egg was inspected carefully before being added to the Easter baskets that I had put out the night before. The Easter bunny had left books, plush toys, pyjamas, and chocolate—so much chocolate. I was desperate to tell Mum the news that Tania had agreed to help me finish my little family, but it could wait. I was having such a lovely morning just watching Rose and Max enjoy such an important first together.

Eventually, I managed to have a shower and get ready for lunch before getting Max down for his morning sleep. Finally, at midday, Mum came downstairs, dressed up and ready to head out for lunch.

The moment she walked in the door, Max popped his head up. Mum hadn't made a sound, but he knew. He had a sense for when his nanna was there. Rose had jumped up immediately, excited to show off all of her eggs as well as all the other goodies that had been left for herself and Max. I had to stop myself from jumping in. I hadn't yet told Rose the news as I hadn't wanted to make the morning about me, but once Mum was inside and sitting down, I told Rose to sit in the playpen with Max because I had something to tell them. Mum looked confused and Rose looked strangely suspicious.

"Tania said yes!" I blurted it out, excitedly.

"You mean with the, you-know-what?" Rose asked, rubbing her non-existent tummy.

Mum looked confused at first, and then, she realised what was going on.

"Oh, Tania? With having the baby?"

"Yep! She and Brendan talked after the picnic last week and they both agreed that they want to help me."

"Oh wow! congratulations. Oh, will you tell the boys at lunch? How long until it's all going to happen?"

"Thanks, chook," I replied, using the pet name that Mum had used for me as a teenager. "It's going to take a couple of months with counselling and all the blood tests and other things."

"Did you hear that, Max?" Rose said if she bounced her little brother on her knee. "You're going to be a big brother."

"What a hilarious thought," Mum said, looking over at me, beaming from ear to ear.

"I don't want to tell the boys yet, I don't want to jinx it after everything that's happened."

"We won't say anything, Mum. It's our little secret."

"I know you won't, baby. On that note, we had better get going."

As I gathered up the nappy bag, jackets, and Max's lunchbox, I knew I could count on my girls to keep it between us for now. There had been so many secrets over the years. My brothers had no idea of the pain and heartbreak, the miscarriages, and the false hopes that came before each one. When I finally told them about my pregnancy with Max, they were both so confused. I said a little prayer to myself then, hoping that I could do it again.

Lunch with my brothers, their families, and our close friends, the Morgans, was lovely. The kids all had a wonderful time with the petting zoo and egg hunt. Even the Easter bunny came for a visit. He looked like he'd had a hard night, actually a hard life. The bunny suit was a little worse for wear, but the kids either didn't notice or they didn't care. He was carrying a big purple basket full of snack-sized chocolates. I joked quietly to Mum that perhaps he was still carrying them around from Halloween. We had a good giggle at the thought.

Everyone had a wonderful day. The kids were exhausted from running around between the carnival rides and the petting zoo. The girls and my nephew Jonathan had a great time sharing chocolate, as did Max.

The day passed in a blur. I caught Rose's eye several times as she winked at me, thoroughly enjoying our little secret. I wondered if my brothers and sister-in-law could see the extra little spring in my step, but Max kept me so busy. Before I knew it, we were packing up and hugging everyone before heading home. Just like the previous couple of nights, Max was pooped and in bed asleep by 7:30 p.m.

Once my little monkey was down for the night, I parked myself on the lounge and pulled up the email from my fertility specialist outlining the steps that Tania would need to go through to start things off.

The first step was for Tania to go through a full blood screening. We had discussed timelines at our picnic and so I knew that she was going along a few days later for the blood tests. The next thing we needed to do was arrange counselling sessions. We would each need to do an individual session—Tania and Brendan would have a session together, and I'd do a solo session. We would then need to do a group session. The group sessions would all be done via Zoom.

The purpose of the counselling sessions was to ensure that all parties involved truly understood what we were getting ourselves into. The counsellor would be interested in what kind of relationship I had with both Tania and Brendan, and what kind of ongoing relationship we would have for the sake of not just the new baby, but also the impact that the process would have on the existing children from both families.

The counselling sessions were a legal requirement that my clinic and any other IVF clinic, at least in New South Wales, were required to conduct when a surrogate or donor was involved with the conception of a baby. I had been through similar counselling sessions a few times because of my use of donor sperm.

Once the first round of blood test results came back, Tania would go for an ultrasound. Those were all standard practice for any woman who was about to have a frozen embryo transfer, or FET for short. I'd asked Tania if she would mind being tested for those NK cells that had caused my miscarriages. Thankfully, she was fine with it. She would do whatever she could to make sure she was able to carry my baby to term.

After the first round of counselling sessions, we would need to wait for another month before doing it all over again—well, the counselling anyway. If we were given the green light from the counsellor, Tania would do another round of blood tests and then we would wait for her next cycle to start so that she could begin the fertility medications. We had discussed how everything would work when we'd had the picnic and a few times since. I loved how excited Tania and Brendan were about helping me finish my family.

Brendan had raised his concerns about giving Tania her hormone injections, but she'd shushed him. She had been a nurse when she was younger, or "in a previous life," as she liked to joke about her life before kids. She assured me that she would be fine to do the injections herself.

When the time came for Tania to have her transfer, I would pick her up from her place and we would head over to my clinic at Bondi. I was thrilled that I'd be in the room at least and that I could say I'd at least been there that day. We were going to go and have a meal in the shopping centre afterwards, just as I'd done the day I'd had little Max transferred as a tiny little embryo.

By the time Mum, the kids, and I boarded the flight up to the Gold Coast, it had been two weeks and one day since Easter. Our trip was originally supposed to be a big family holiday to visit friends and go to Disney World in Orlando, Florida, but between my health issues, losing my job, and my paranoia about taking Max for a simple car ride, let alone such a long flight, we decided that staying with Mum's best friend on the Gold Coast was a safer bet. If everything went well, then we agreed to take the kids to the US the following year.

Tania and I spoke most days while we were away and most days more than once, especially if we'd had a counselling appointment that day. We got the news that Tania's blood tests had all come back normal and the counsellor hadn't detected any red flags that would concern him. He was impressed by the amount of research that each of us had done about surrogacy in Australia and was happy with the frank and open discussions we'd had about our expectations, about the way we would plan to become an extension of each other's families.

Tania, Brendan, and I all agreed that, should the embryo transfer result in a baby, we would foster a cousin relationship for our children, not just for the new baby, but the four children we already had between us. The fact that Tania and Brendan lived in Hunters Hill, just a matter of minutes down the road from Lane Cove, meant that being in each other's lives was going to be easy. A lot of people chose a more distant relationship, but I wanted my baby to grow up surrounded by everyone who loved them. I felt honoured to know that they wanted to take on that role. It reminded me, not for the first time, what a wonderful eclectic little mix of people I got to call family.

It was surprising to hear that it wasn't rare for people to get to this stage of their surrogacy journey without having had those frank discussions. I couldn't believe that people could go into such a serious and life-changing commitment without making sure they were on the same page.

The week in Queensland was fun. We hired a car since we were staying with our friends out in Tallebudgera, a suburb about twenty minutes west of the coast. The kids swam every day, even Max had a wonderful time trying out his fancy floaty from the Easter bunny.

Tania and Brendan had taken their girls to see Brendan's mum in Perth. They were keen to go on a holiday now before she was pregnant. I loved that Tania was so excited about helping me. She was one of those people who loved being pregnant. There had been no morning sickness with her girls, and she'd been back in her jeans within ten days both times. I chuckled as I thought about the maternity jeans I was still wearing the winter after having Rose. I'd done the same thing with a pair of maternity tracksuit pants after having Max, but they had been huge on me after a couple of months. It hadn't stopped me from wearing them, though; they were the only pants that didn't hurt my tender stomach in those first few months.

I shuddered to think about that. I was so thankful that Jack had come along and fixed my injuries once and for all. I was still having a bit of discomfort in my tummy and my groin most days, but it was minimal. I wouldn't go as far as to call it pain, and it was a million times better than it had been back in September when the prolapse had been discovered. I now snuggled my baby without a second thought, which was absolutely glorious.

Chapter 10
May 2023

May arrived again before I knew it. On the second weekend, we celebrated Mum's birthday and Mother's Day, and then a week-and-a-bit later it was Max's turn. I had excitedly prepared a small smash cake for him. It was a naked cake, with a vanilla sponge and blue and white ombré icing. Rose had taken great pride in painting a number one cake topper in a medium shade of blue that went perfectly with the icing.

After dinner, Max was happily playing with his new toys. He'd had a wonderful time opening gifts: a plush crocodile, bath toys, and a baby TV remote control, among several other things. It was getting close to bath time, so after getting my birthday boy all sorted on the picnic blanket with Rose to keep him from crawling off into the garden, I raced inside and grabbed the cake from the kitchen bench. The moment it was placed in front of him, Mum and I grabbed our phones to film the fun. As I had expected, Max absolutely immersed himself in the cake.

Within moments, it was all over his face, in his hair, and in his ear. He even managed to get a little bit in his mouth. To say that he loved it was a definite understatement. I couldn't believe my tiny little baby was already one year-old.

Once Rose and Max were in bed for the evening, I finally had a chance to sit down and reflect on the past year. There had been so many lows in those early months, the pain, the operations, the distress I felt about my baby not bonding with me the way I had so desperately wanted him to. I'd made it out the other end, though, and I couldn't have been happier and more in love with my babies.

Tania, Brendan, and the girls were planning to attend Max's birthday party, on the Saturday after his birthday. We had been in constant contact, and I knew that she was due to get the last round of blood test results back in the next day or two. It was the last hurdle before she was able to start the cycle. I couldn't believe that by Max's birthday the following year, all going to plan, Max would no longer be the baby of the family. It was wild to think that my baby could be a big brother.

The sound of my phone snapped me out of my daydream. It was Tania; her ears must have been burning, I thought to myself with a smile.

The message just read, "Hey babe, can you talk?" It didn't occur to me at the time that her message was anything other than normal. I'd responded that I could. I figured that she must have something to check with me since we weren't expecting the blood tests to come back so soon. The moment that Tania answered her phone, I could tell she'd been crying.

"Hi," she said, sniffing.

"Is everything okay? Are Brendan and the girls okay?" I asked frantically.

"I am so sorry. I don't know how it happened," she burst into tears. I was so confused.

"What's going on, hun?"

"I'm pregnant," Tania said through her sobs.

"What do you mean?" I asked dumbly. I didn't understand; how could she be pregnant? The transfer wasn't going to be for another few weeks. But like a lightning bolt, slamming into my heart and shattering it like glass, I realised what was happening.

Nothing made sense. Brendan had had a vasectomy. They'd been very open about it when we'd had the discussion at the park, weeks earlier. I knew that there would be a pregnancy test done, among other things like STD screening, when the blood tests were taken. I'd had those blood tests a million times myself, before so many of my failed cycles. Not once had my dream of a miraculous positive test come true, but now, the one time I needed that test to be negative, it wasn't—it bloody well wasn't!

I felt numb. I didn't know what to say. I was devastated for myself. I felt like I'd just lost my baby before they had even had a chance to try and exist. I knew it was selfish, but at that moment I didn't care. I wanted to scream. I wanted to scream, and sob, and punch something. It took me a moment to realise that Tania was waiting for me to say something.

"Oh. I don't. Okay." I didn't know what to say. "Can we talk tomorrow?"

"Of course, I'm so sorry, babe."

"I know," I said quietly before ending the call.

My lungs closed. I had been asthmatic as a child and would feel a tightness in my chest, knowing that I needed to use my puffer, but this was different. In the moments after I ended that fateful call, I could have died. I surely would have, under different circumstances, had I not had two precious children asleep just metres away. I had a stash of paper bags in my pantry, left over from the nasty asthma attacks I'd suffered from for months after my first bout of Covid. After a couple of minutes, the paper bag made me feel better, or able to breathe again.

Max's birthday party was two days away. I had hired one of the marquees at the Diddy, a local bowling club that we sometimes wandered down to for a meal. I had forty-three people coming from all over Sydney to celebrate my little boy's birthday. I had so much fun planning everything: the lolly bags, the dinosaur decorations, and the cake. I had chosen an adorable first birthday outfit for Max, and Rose and I had dresses to match. They'd been custom-made and had cost a small fortune.

In the moments after my call with Tania, after my little panic attack had subsided, I pondered how on earth was I supposed to face Tania? I couldn't exactly uninvite her from the party, and I didn't want to. I had watched countless friends give birth to beautiful babies over the years whilst I was so desperately trying to have my little boy. I was always happy for my friends, but this was different. I was supposed to be the one getting another baby. I didn't want anything to ruin my baby's special day. I had to do something to take away the burning feeling in my chest and the rapid heartbeat.

I did three things. Two of those things were a great idea. First, I climbed into bed with my babies. Rose had climbed into my bed to give Max birthday goodnight kisses and ended up falling asleep. I gently moved her over and kissed her on the back of the head. She mumbled something and then went straight back to sleep.

Next, I kissed my sweet boy on his little head. He had almost a full head of that beautiful golden hair. I loved rubbing my chin crease over his fluffy little head; it was like kissing a thousand little ducks. Being with my babies had an immediate calming effect, as did messaging Lindsay to tell her what had happened.

Patience isn't a virtue that I had been blessed with. I had joked about it often enough, but I knew that it was true. I needed a plan B immediately. I couldn't possibly get so close and give up on my baby. That's why, five minutes after messaging Lindsay, when there was no response, I decided to go back to my original plan: to send the letters that I had written all those weeks earlier. I immediately pulled up the drafts on my phone where I had saved them, ready to hit send.

I decided at that moment that the next person I would contact would be my friend Josephine. Without a second thought, I pulled up the email that I had written for her, changed a few dates, and hit send. If Tania couldn't do it for me, then I would find someone else who would help me have my baby. I was sure that I was going to have another boy, and I needed to get cracking. I wanted my last two babies to be as close in age as possible.

I've often thought that Lindsay, Chelsea, and I had some kind of otherworldly connection. Not ten seconds after I hit send on Josephine's email, I received a reply from Lindsay. She wanted to make sure I was okay. My friend was devastated for me. She didn't understand how it had happened, apart from the basics of the birds and bees. Only one of my very best friends could have made me laugh at that moment.

Once she was sure that I was okay, Lindsay wanted to know what parts of the process I had been through already. I went through it all. There should have been a counselling session the following Tuesday and then Tania would have been ready to start the hormone injections to get ready for the embryo to be transferred about a month later. I couldn't believe the unfairness of it. I really thought I was going to have my baby in my arms. How the hell was I going to tell Mum and Rose? They were going to be devastated. I thought of all the times Rose had thought she was finally getting a baby brother or sister over the years, only to learn that I had had another miscarriage. I gulped back my sob at the thought, trying not to wake her up.

I realised then that I was going to have to call my fertility clinic the next day and give them the news that the cycle was off. Of course, they had known about it before I did. They were the ones who had told Tania she needed to tell me ASAP. I just wished that it didn't need to be on my baby's birthday.

Lindsay and I had been messaging back and forth for a while when I realised that it was almost 11 pm. I knew that she would normally have been asleep. Eleanor was almost three months old and was already sleeping four-to-five-hour stretches at night but I remembered all too well how important it was to sleep while the baby did. I was still trying to stick to that rule myself because even though Max was a good little sleeper, he was also an early bird. We had a family of kookaburras in a nearby gum tree who would start their malarkey anywhere between 5 am and 6 am. Max often woke up from the sounds of them and so I knew that it was time for me to get some sleep too.

We signed off with a promise to chat the following day. Lindsay and her sister Chelsea had some tasks that they had insisted on helping with for the party, including doughnut stands and a huge blow-up dinosaur costume that Cam was going to nip out and change into before the cake was brought out. I went to sleep that night thinking about the wonderful adventure that we would be celebrating for the beautiful baby I already had, but with a heavy heart, feeling the same way I had all those times before when my hopes of having Max had once again ended in heartbreak.

I woke up early the following morning, before Rose and Max. I was happily lying in bed searching through my emails and procrastinating about getting up, when suddenly I remembered my conversation from the night before. It didn't sting quite as much in the light of the new day. I guess I had developed a thick skin through all those years. I knew that I was going to have to talk to Tania again, though, and I was dreading it. But I had so much to do to get ready for Max's party the following day. I had always loved planning parties, especially when they were for my children. I knew that I had no choice but to do what I had learned throughout my infertility journey and that was to get up and show up. And so once the kids were awake, I turned on the Wiggles on my bedroom TV, put Max in his cot, and headed for the shower.

Rose had been given the day off school. I had resisted at first, but she had been asking for the day off for weeks. She wanted to help get everything ready for the party, so eventually, I agreed. This was her first day off for the year. It was already term two, and she was killing it at school. By lunch time, we had gotten a massive amount of the food cooked and packed away. The kids were having lunch when my phone rang. As soon as I saw Josephine's name on the screen, I knew what she was calling about.

I answered the phone with the usual amount of enthusiasm. I loved that woman; we'd had some fun and wild times back when we worked together, long before either of us became mums. After a few minutes spent catching up, Josephine raised the subject of the email I'd sent the night before. We had never discussed our birth stories before, and so I was shocked and saddened to hear that Josephine had been living with some of the same injuries that I had sustained during Max's birth a year earlier. Her kids were eleven and eight. Josephine had planned to have four children but her doctor had cautioned her against it. The prolapse she had sustained during her younger son's birth was nowhere near as bad as mine but it would become more severe if she were to carry another baby.

Her doctor had advised her that, should she go ahead with another pregnancy, she would need to have a caesarean for the birth. After two years of trying for another baby, my friend had realised that she actually didn't want to be married to her children's father anymore, and so she had eventually divorced him and made peace with the fact that she might not get to have any more babies. She explained that she was still hoping, deep down, that somehow she would manage to have at least one more child.

Josephine wasn't anywhere near ready to give up on her dream of having another baby. I completely understood and appreciated her candour, that she valued me enough as a friend to pick up the phone and talk to me. I was disappointed, of course, but mostly I was full of love and appreciation for my friend. She asked if we were good. We were, we were better than ever. I told her that I couldn't wait to see her, her sister, and their kids the following day.

As I hung up, I realised it was probably time to face the next conversation that I needed to have. I had walked outside to take the call with Josephine. I could see the kids in the kitchen; Max was in his high chair still eating his croissant. I tapped Tania's name in my recent call log and after just two rings, the phone answered. Brendan had seen my name and thought he'd better answer.

"Hey," Brendan's voice was faint, almost as if he was distant from the phone.

"Hey, Brendan," I answered, feeling self-conscious for the first time since meeting him.

I heard Tania's voice as she approached. She sounded just as apprehensive as I felt. Her words were muffled before she took the phone from her husband.

"Hello."

"Hey, hun, I thought we should probably talk," I said, trying to keep the emotion out of my voice as the tears threatened again.

"I'm so sorry, I don't know how this has happened. Bren's had the chop. This wasn't meant to happen." I realised that she was crying again and knew I had to let her off the hook somehow. I realised it wasn't all about me.

"We don't want to come and ruin Max's birthday, but I would like to drop a present over while you're out tomorrow." Tania sounded so sad, which made me feel even worse.

"No, please don't do that. I can get over this. I know you didn't do it on purpose." It was the first time I had really acknowledged that fact, even to myself.

"You guys are so important to me. To us. Please come tomorrow?"

"Are you sure?" she asked, apprehensively.

"Yes. To be honest, it's the only thing I am completely sure about right now."

We agreed that we would talk about the appointments that needed to be cancelled on Monday. For that day and the weekend ahead, I just wanted to celebrate my little boy's birthday. Everything else could wait.

Chapter 11
Late May 2023

When I was a child, my mum used to say that the weather people picked the forecast out of a hat. It was still a running joke in my family whenever the forecast was wrong. Thankfully, that Saturday in late-May was just such a day. It was supposed to be bucketing down for most of the day, but instead there was barely a cloud in the sky. By 11 am, it was 23 degrees. It was the perfect autumn day.

We arrived half an hour before the guests were due. Mum, Rose, Max, and I made our way over to the marquee we had reserved for the afternoon to start getting everything set up. As usual, I had a plan. Mum would give Max his milk whilst Rose and I brought everything in from the car. There were boxes of decorations and sweets including the doughnuts, fairy bread, and the cute dinosaur cake that Rose had designed to match the invites she'd made a few weeks earlier.

Everything went according to plan. The party looked like it had been professionally staged, thanks to Rose and Lindsay. I often tried to convince Lindsay to set up a party business. She was so great at making things look next level, unlike me. I wasn't sure where Rose got her artistic talents, but I had no problem with admitting that it hadn't come from me.

The guests started arriving right on time, and by 12:15 pm, our big white marquee, or "the tent" as we'd quickly nicknamed it, was bustling with excited friends, aunts, uncles, and cousins, all keen to see the birthday boy. Max was dressed to the nines in his little outfit that matched mine and Rose's dresses. He was beside himself with excitement. I had no doubt that my boy knew that the fanfare was all in his honour.

The afternoon went far too quickly. The bigger kids had a great time running around the lawn right in front of us, and eventually, we hired some green space so that they could have a barefoot bowl. Some of the adults even joined in and it was such a lot of fun. The food was plentiful and amazing as I'd come to expect from our little local club.

And then, just when I thought he couldn't possibly get any more excited, Lindsay and Rose carried the cake out, and my little Max squealed with delight. He was fascinated by the candles, just as he had been two days earlier, and he was delighted by all of the grownups and the big and little kids alike singing to him. He jumped up and down on my knee and then clapped along with everyone else when Rose helped him blow out his candle.

Once again, Max was given some cake. It was just a small piece, but he had a wonderful time rubbing it on his face and hair. I noticed a couple of disapproving looks from women walking past, but I didn't care. I'd had fought so hard to have my beautiful boy, and if he wanted to smoosh cake in his hair or eat the whole damn piece, it was okay by me. At that moment, he could have stomped the darn thing with his feet, and I wouldn't have been bothered.

Oh, and speaking of fighting hard to have my baby—and indeed babies—Tania and Brendan had showed up with the girls as promised. The only people who knew about my search for a surrogate were Josepine, Chelsea, Lindsay, Mum, and Rose. The only person, other than Josephine, who knew about the latest development was Lindsay, and I knew she wouldn't treat my new friends any differently now.

I felt Tania's relief when I hugged her to say hello. At first, she started to apologise again, but I shushed her. I hadn't told Mum and Rose the news about her pregnancy, and I didn't want my friend to feel guilty about her little baby. I was a big believer in fate and I'd always believed that things happened for a reason, even if that reason wasn't always immediately clear. I had no idea where to go next in my quest to have my last baby, but Tania's baby, that unexpected little surprise, was meant to be. I was happy for her and her little family despite my own sadness and confusion. I really believed that I would still get my turn when the time was right. I sure as hell wasn't ready to give up on my dream.

The party was a great success. Rose handed out the lolly bags to the other children as they left. Max was so tired that he fell asleep in his pram as soon as I put him in there. I had planned to race around cleaning and packing the car, but with Mum wheeling him slowly around the outer edge of the green, I was able to take my time getting everything packed and cleaned away. I hadn't had time to eat whilst the party was happening, so finally managed to grab a couple of pieces of leftover pizza that someone had boxed up for me to take home. There was even a single lonely piece of fairy bread left. I picked it up and stuffed the whole thing in my mouth, vowing to make a couple more pieces when I got home.

Lindsay had been helping me clean up, but eventually, the kids started to get cranky. Little Eleanor had been changed and fed but desperately needed a sleep. Cam suggested taking the kids for a drive so that they could sleep and then coming back to get Lindsay, but I wasn't having a bar of that. They had done so much to help me get ready, and the last thing I wanted was for them to have overtired children screaming the place down when they got home. I insisted they get the kids in the car and head off. I thanked them both a dozen times before they left. Lindsay had told me earlier that she had something she wanted to talk to me about, but we hadn't found the time throughout the hectic afternoon. As the kids were loaded into the car, we made a plan to catch up the following weekend at either my place or Balmoral Beach, depending on the weather.

Just a few minutes after Lindsay and Cam had driven off with three sleepy kids in the back, Max woke up, right in time for his afternoon bottle. I had brought a flask of milk in case we were still there. He drank it down with his usual level of enthusiasm. Everyone but our little household had left by then and so once

Max's milk had settled for a few minutes, we all piled into the car and drove the five minutes home.

I couldn't believe we had finished celebrating my little boy's birthday. It was surreal to think about where I had been a year earlier. I had just had my tiny little boy with his impossibly skinny legs and his sweet soft, bald little head. I had absolutely no idea what was waiting around the corner at the time. I loved my baby more than life. And my Rose. There were no words to express my love and gratitude for that amazing child. As I watched my babies playing on the well-loved rug, I vowed again that somehow I was going to have my last baby. I had no idea how, but I knew that I was not done trying.

Chapter 12
A week later

The party had been everything I'd imagined and so much more, thanks to all our wonderful family and friends. My friend Tina and the rest of her family, the Morgans, had a great time catching up with my brothers and the rest of the school gang. Mum, Rose, Chelsea, Lindsay, and Cam had done so much work to help me get ready, and during one of our chats in the days that followed, we agreed that as long as the weather held out, we would meet up for an early dinner at Balmoral beach. Balmoral was our favourite beach since we had our kids. The plan was to grab pizzas on the way and then have a picnic. It was a tradition. Much like my little family's tradition of the carpet picnic, we would set up our blankets and towels on the sand and then lay out all sorts of snacks to share.

Cam usually went and played and splashed about with the kids whilst Lindsay and I sat and talked. We hadn't been down to Balmoral since I was pregnant with Max and so we were excited to be planning our little dinner.

Lindsay and I checked in most nights, just as we had done for many years. Sometimes life would get too busy, but for the most part, we had some kind of contact each day. The week between

Max's birthday party and our beach picnic was no different. We chatted every night once all the babies were in bed. Lindsay had been so supportive once again about my decision to try for my last baby. She knew that If I hadn't ended up with the devastating injuries that had left me unable to carry another child, I would have had my last little frosty baby transferred a few months earlier.

When I found out that I was pregnant with Max, I decided that I would use my last embryo when he was about six months old, meaning that my two youngest children would be born about eighteen months apart. Starting the process when Max was six months old meant that he would likely be about eight or nine months by the time I actually had the embryo transfer, because of the immune protocol that included several weeks of medications beforehand. Lindsay knew about my plans. She'd had a similar plan for her last two babies, but it had taken longer than expected to get pregnant, so Harrison and Eleanor ended up being three years apart. My friend had faced many challenges in the process of bringing her babies into the world, but thankfully she had never had to go down the path of IVF.

Never having been through IVF meant that other than what she'd been told by friends or what she'd seen on TV, Lindsay didn't know much about how everything worked. She was still fascinated by the whole process. When we talked at night, our chats always seemed to involve how everything worked. From whether the needles hurt, which thankfully, I would explain to her, they didn't—for the most part anyway. The exception was the progesterone in oil injections. Those things were huge and made you want to scream, especially when you accidentally gave yourself a cork thigh as I had done a couple of times with Max. I joked that I'd invented a few new swear words whilst administering those nasty injections. I'd only needed to use a handful of the PIO injections, thankfully, and they were just a precaution because of the heavy bleed I'd had early on.

The funny thing about IVF, I realised as I was talking through the process with Lindsay, was that once you were actually pregnant, everything basically proceeded the same way as any other pregnancy did. You had your seven-week scan, called the viability scan, then the twelve-week scan. If you were going to get morning sickness, the way you got pregnant had no bearing on that. I had exactly the same experience with both of my children, despite them having been conceived very differently .

The baby growing inside of you would still be the size of a grape, followed by an avocado, and then a watermelon. Or at least you'd feel like you were carrying a watermelon by the end. That didn't change regardless of whether you'd had a tiny little embryo inserted into your uterus or you'd had a roll in the hay. The end result was the same.

"You *are* going to have your third baby, you know," Lindsay told me one evening when I called her.

"I just feel so sad. Maybe I really am only supposed to have two children." I was really starting to feel like the universe was telling me to quit while I was ahead.

"Hey, I knew that you were going to have Max. Even when you wanted to give up, I just knew."

"I nearly gave up so many times, but you convinced me to keep going. I'm so glad I listened to you." I genuinely loved her for pushing me.

"Trust me, okay?" She sounded so sure. I couldn't help but feel the same way.

By Friday night, we had planned all the food and checked the weather a million times, but when I woke up on Saturday morning, I was still relieved to see that the sun was already shining through the window. Max was fast asleep. It always occurred to me how tiny he looked when he was asleep. It took everything I had not to squeeze his chunky little legs, but before I had a chance to think any more about those thighs, my cheeky little dolly started to stir.

Rose had been woken by the noisy neighbourhood kookaburras as well and had tiptoed in, which was pointless really, since our floorboards creaked loudly regardless of how much care you took. Once Max was awake and everyone had had big kisses and cuddles, I hopped out of bed to start off the morning routine. That day was like any other Saturday. We had decided not to enrol Rose in her singing and acting classes for terms one and two of the school year. I had wanted her to explore a new sport with school. She had chosen touch footy, which suited me perfectly since the games were played at 8:30 am every week. Having the games early meant that we could be back before Max woke from his morning sleep. On the odd occasion that Mum wasn't feeling up to looking after him, he would simply come with us and sleep through the game in his pram or the carrier that he was already growing out of.

That morning, Mum was feeling good. She had improved tenfold since her Meniere's relapse and seemed to be back in remission, except for the occasional day when she felt a bit dizzy. It was such a relief to see my mum returning to her old self and able to play with Max again. When Rose and I walked through the gate after footy, we were greeted by mum and our little mate. Max had woken up about fifteen minutes earlier, so they'd headed outside to enjoy the unseasonably warm day. It had been so warm and sunny for weeks. Autumn had gotten lost on the way to our beautiful little corner of the world. It was very different to the year before, when Max was brand new. The cold at the time had been unbearable. The warm weather was so much nicer. It was the perfect day for an afternoon beach picnic.

After a lovely lunch in the garden and then another big sleep for Max, we finally jumped in the car, ready to head off on our little adventure. We left home early. We had ordered pizzas from my friend's Italian restaurant, Attimo. They didn't actually open to the public until 5 pm, but David was always happy to have our food ready a bit earlier. We arrived at the restaurant just before 4 pm to grab the food before continuing on to Balmoral.

We pulled into the car park just twenty minutes later and headed over to the playground where we had agreed to meet. As we approached the gate, I spotted Lindsay sitting on a park bench right next to the fence. Within a few minutes of catching her attention, we were setting up our picnic blankets on the grass, right next to the sand.

The bigger kids ran around with Rose's hot pink football whilst Lindsay, Cam, and I got the food all set up before calling them over for dinner. As the kids ate their pizza, I grabbed the nibbles from my esky. I fed Max while Lindsay sorted out a bottle for Eleanor, and Cam joined the kids in devouring the pizzas. Watching them all hoe in made me glad that we had ordered more than we needed. Even Max turned his nose up at his vegetables. He knew that what everyone else was eating looked far tastier, and he wasn't disappointed when I gave in and handed him the slice that I had been about to tuck into myself.

Once the bigger kids had finished eating, they were keen to get up and play with the football again. Cam had no choice but to leave the last of his own food when the boys jumped on him, insisting that they needed even numbers for their game. Once Eleanor had finished her milk and been burped, and Max had finally given in and eaten three mouthfuls of veggies and a few pieces of fruit, we swapped babies. It was crazy how quickly all of our children were growing up, but the babies in particular seemed to have shot up even in the week since Max's birthday party. We happily cuddled each other's little monkeys as we chatted about what busy year it had already been.

The kids soon got tired of playing with the football. The boys had a lot more energy than Rose, who was feeling a little sore and sorry for herself from the morning's game. Especially Harrison who'd had a lovely time being the boss of the Rabboh's, as he called them. Eventually, Cam walked over and mumbled something to Lindsay, but she shooed him away. She asked him to take the boys to search for shells. Rose was keen to join them. I watched with so much pride as my girl gently led the boys along the sand, with the water lapping gently at their feet. She helped Cam ensure they didn't get their clothes wet, scooping them up easily if the water came too close. The boys excitedly showed their dad and their special big girl, Rose, each shell that they found before placing it back onto the sand. As the shell-collecting expedition continued in front of us, Lindsay asked if I had ever heard back from my cousin. It had been several weeks since I'd sent the email asking if she would consider helping me to have my last baby. It was so strange. I had never heard anything, not a peep. I thought that eventually my cousin would reply, but nothing. There was just silence. I filled Lindsay in on Tania's latest news as well.

The level of HCG, the pregnancy hormone that was detected in the blood test, was so high for Tania. The level was something like 32,000. I had been several weeks pregnant before I had levels that high with Max. Tania's first round of blood tests had included a beta HCG pregnancy test as well and that one was negative. The doctors realised that she must have fallen pregnant within days of that first test. Or she was already pregnant but the levels were not high enough to be detected by the test. Tania was going to need to have a dating scan so that they could figure out how far along she was in her pregnancy. It made me think about that Alanis Morissette song. It truly was ironic.

Lindsay wanted to know then if I had anyone else that I was planning to ask. I remembered a little sadly what I had realised a few days earlier. Unless I met another stranger that I connected with, I probably wasn't realistically going to have another baby after all. I couldn't ask my younger cousin Carrie because it would be too weird after not hearing back from her sister. I had found out from Nick that he and Skye had decided to finally take the sabbatical that they'd been planning for a long time. They had been working fourteen-hour days for the past several years and taking turns studying for just as long.

My little brother had earned top honours in his MBA whilst also working in his high-powered job. Skye had then gone on and done the same. She was turning forty a couple of weeks after our picnic and the trip had just been locked in. They would be leaving in late February the following year and spending roughly nine months living abroad in France whilst visiting several other countries that they loved in Europe. The trip was an absolute dream come true for them both and I knew that there was no way I could ask my sister-in-law. It wasn't an option. It was starting to seem like no one was.

I answered a few more questions about what it entailed to be a surrogate .

"What happens with the blood crossing over from the surrogate to the baby?" Lindsay asked, looking fascinated.

"I used to think that blood crossed over too, but it doesn't," I replied, feeling like an expert on the subject after my months of research.

"And does the embryo transfer hurt?"

"It really doesn't." I explained, having been through the process a few times before. "It's not even as bad as a pap-smear to be honest."

"And you just go into hospital for the day, do you?" she asked, looking almost concerned.

"No. it is literally a five-minute process. I sat in the food court at Bondi Junction for almost an hour after the transfer that resulted in Max. I sat there eating a cupcake of all things and wondered if I was imagining it. My doctor didn't even use an ultrasound wand to guide the embryo. I was sure it wouldn't work."

"But it did!" Lindsay explained excitedly as she tickled Max, much to his delight.

I had to laugh at the craziness of it all. I had been on the IVF roller coaster for so long that none of it seemed strange to me anymore, but I could see how it would all be so strange and surreal to someone who had never been through fertility treatments.

I reminded my friend that I could only talk to the physical side of IVF. The emotional side of growing a new life inside of you and knowing that you had to give that baby to someone else to raise wasn't something I had any idea about. I couldn't tell her the first thing about that side of it. I had thought once that I would be a surrogate for someone else before I found myself with those injuries that had changed things forever. I realised at that moment that I'd never really thought about what it would mean to carry a baby that wasn't mine. It would take a truly remarkable woman to give such a gift to someone else.

My thoughts drifted off to a place where I was pregnant with my third child. I would have done anything to feel one last baby moving inside of me. It struck me for the millionth time how unfair it was that I could no longer do what was supposed to come naturally to a woman, all because of some doctor who had used a pair of forceps incorrectly and then left chunks of my son's placenta inside of me, causing an infection so nasty that I'd needed intravenous antibiotics to get it under control.

I would take the morning sickness, the reflux, and the carpal tunnel that I'd experienced with Max a million times over if I could. But I couldn't. Another pregnancy could kill both me and my unborn baby. My thoughts were interrupted by Lindsay's voice. I looked up to see her staring at the kids who were once again playing football on the grass with Cam.

"Sorry, chick, I was just thinking about the unfairness of it all. I was a million miles away," I said, trying not to spoil our lovely little picnic.

"I'll do it," Lindsay said simply, looking a little nervous suddenly.

"Do what?" I was confused, wondering if I had missed something while my thoughts were spinning around a minute earlier.

"I'll carry your baby for you. I'll be your surrogate." She said, looking straight at me. We'd swapped babies back a few minutes earlier and she was kissing Eleanor on the head as she waited for the penny to drop.

"What? Really? Oh wow. Oh my gosh!" I knew that I was raising my voice. Max squealed along with me, excited about what he'd just heard despite not understanding it. "Are you sure?"

"I am. Cam and I have been talking about it since you found out you were going to need a surrogate. We both agreed that if you hadn't found anyone by the time I gave birth to Elly, we would help you. Then Tania came along before I had a chance to offer to help."

"Oh my gosh." I cried as I hugged my beautiful friend. "Oh. Wow. Thank you!" I didn't know what else to say.

Lindsay explained that she and Cam had discussed the idea of her carrying my baby for me several months earlier, long before I connected with Tania. They had done a lot of research on the subject, even joining one of the same social media groups that I was a part of in order to learn more about the process. Lindsay had spoken with her GP about what tests needed to be done. Everything looked good and my dear friend had been building up the courage to offer her help when I'd met Tania. Lindsay was so thrilled for me when I told her about Tania. She hadn't wanted to make me feel like I had to choose and so she had happily stepped back, just wanting to support me. Once

Tania had shared her unexpected baby news, Lindsay once again spoke with Cam. He was still 100% onboard.

"Oh my gosh. Thank you. You guys are amazing."

I truly didn't know what else to say. I couldn't begin to describe the way I felt at that moment when I finally started to understand what Lindsay was offering to do. Carry my baby for me. I had never been proposed to by the love of my life, but I could imagine that the feeling would be something like that. Pure joy, love, and hope for the future. I jumped up again and hugged her, this time putting Max down carefully on the picnic blanket first. He looked very confused but thoroughly amused as well. I guess it was strange to see his mummy laughing and crying and jumping around. By this point the kids were all visibly confused. They were hurrying back to the picnic blankets and enquiring about our well-being.

Cam walked up behind the kids and I jumped up once again, this time hugging him. I didn't want to say anything to Rose until we knew that we could go ahead with everything. My sweet daughter had been on such a roller coaster over the years. By the time I had gotten pregnant with Max, she truly believed that we were never going to get our little baby. But we had, and she was so in love with her baby brother. I was sure that there was no little boy in the history of little boys that could possibly have had a more loving and attentive big sister. I so desperately wanted our last baby to join our little family, but I'd tell Rose if and when things progressed. With that in mind, I thanked Cam. He immediately understood the strange side glance I'd made towards my girl. Cam was a good man and knew what it meant to put your kids first.

Chapter 13
June 2023

We packed everyone up and headed to the cars not long after Cam and the kids came over to find out what the crazy lady, aka me, was doing jumping around and squealing. Rose, bless her ever-hopeful little heart, had asked me quite seriously if we'd finally won the lotto. I'd never really been one to gamble, but I had been playing the same numbers every week for a couple of years. Ever since Covid got me thinking about the mansion I would like to have been locked in, instead of our lovely but small granny flat. I often loved to fantasise about the house we would build with our winnings, not to mention the ridiculous cars I would buy.

In a way, I thought, I might be going to win the lottery for the third time. But I didn't tell Rose that. I just told her that we had been planning a couple of things including the trip the following summer. Luckily, my little Miss, who was just a matter of weeks away from becoming a teenager, had in recent months come to the conclusion that I was a bit odd. And so, she just shrugged and put on a Taylor Swift song. Rose had orders to keep Max from falling asleep whilst I drove home, and she did, just.

Once we were home and the kids had been bathed, I got Max into bed. He took just a few minutes to get to sleep, which was almost unheard of for him. Lindsay and I had agreed to chat about the next steps once the kids were in bed. I knew that I would probably be home twenty minutes before Lindsay, Cam, and the kids, and so once my little ducky was asleep, I decided that the first thing I needed to do was to once again let my fertility specialist know that I may have found a surrogate. I knew that the email was unlikely to be seen for close to twelve hours, but I didn't care. I was eager to start things off.

The next thing I did was message Lindsay. I had sent a huge thank you gif followed by a little message about how grateful I was to her, no matter what happened from there. Once the message had been sent from my phone, I slowly slipped out of bed, careful not to wake Max.

I didn't like leaving Max alone in my bed even if he was asleep. He was quite proficient with his crawling ability by that point. He was getting very close to walking and it terrified me that he could fall and hurt himself. With that in mind, I quickly raced to my office. I grabbed my laptop and then tiptoed back to bed, only stopping on the way to grab the last few pieces of Caramilk chocolate out of the fridge, thinking that the diet could wait until tomorrow.

I sat quietly at the end of the bed and laid out the laptop. Lindsay hadn't written back yet, so I hopped into my email. I searched for the email from the solicitors and opened the forms that had all been signed many weeks before by Tania,

Brendan, and myself, as well as our lawyers. The forms had seemed like a minor detail then, but suddenly they were so very important. I wanted to refresh my memory so that I could make sure that my friends truly understood what they were getting themselves into.

The legalities of surrogacy differ depending on which state of Australia you live in. Living in NSW meant that both single women and gay couples were allowed to use a surrogate. I had been utterly appalled when I had first read about the laws in some other states regarding who was or was not allowed to seek a surrogate. If a woman was seeking a surrogate, she had to provide a medical report stating that she was unable to carry a child herself. I had that very report attached to the forms that had been signed by my specialist, Jack. I could see myself reading that report twenty years in the future. I knew that it would always make me catch my breath, reading the words that I'd been told half a dozen times: that it wasn't safe for me to carry another baby because of the damage I had sustained from those forceps.

The biggest factor that spooked a lot of people was that the surrogate woman and her partner, if she had one, would legally be considered as the child's parents until the final step, the adoption process, was complete. Finding a close friend or family member drastically reduced the risk that the surrogate would feel too connected to the child to be able to give them up.

If the surrogate decided that they couldn't part with the baby, they were legally allowed to keep them. The biological parents already had to go through the lengthy and expensive process of gaining custody of their child through the courts to formally adopt them. But there are no precedents set in Australia because there are so few surrogate births here.

I had built such a wonderful friendship with Tania. We had hit it off the moment we first met, but Lindsay, Chelsea, and their kids were already an extension of my family. They, like the Morgans, were the family I had chosen for myself. I had so much history with those women, history that spanned decades. We had laughed and cried together. We'd had crazy nights on the town and countless evenings sitting in my car down at Woolwhich ferry wharf whilst we ate pizza and pondered all manner of things. We'd driven for hours to cheer the Rabbitohs on together and cuddled each other's newborn babies. I had more in common with Chelsea and Lindsay than I did with some members of my extended family. I couldn't think of anyone I would rather have carry my baby safely into this world than my dear friend.

And speaking of Lindsay, it had been a good half an hour or so since I'd messaged her. I checked, and sure enough, she was online and writing a message. I watched those three dots bounce around my screen for a minute or so before her message appeared.

Lindsay started by thanking me for the lovely afternoon and evening. The boys had talked about Rose collecting shells and letting them play with her big pink football all the way home. Max had been a hit as usual; he had been more eager than ever to try and keep up with the boys when we first sat down. The bigger boys didn't consider Max to be the baby anymore. Their sister was now the baby of the group. And speaking of which, I messaged Lindsay back then, asking if she was sure that it was something that she could truly do?

As it turned out, my friend, my sister from another mister, had first had the idea soon after I'd found out that I wouldn't be allowed to carry my last baby. That had been the previous September when Max was just a few months old. Lindsay would have been just three or four months pregnant with Eleanor then, and yet she had already been thinking about doing something so wonderful for me and for my little family.

Cam had been on board right from the start. Of course, he had some reservations about Lindsay going through a fourth pregnancy. She had turned forty a few months earlier, placing her at the upper end of the preferred age range set by my doctor. Regarding the time she would need off work to recover from the birth, my friends already had someone working a five-day fortnight to cover for Lindsay while she was on maternity leave. She wasn't planning to go back to work for at least a year. Eleanor was her last baby, after all, and she wanted to spend every possible moment just enjoying her baby. I could completely understand that. I was doing the same thing with Max. It was just out of this world to think that my sweet boy was one year old. I was having trouble coping with Rose being in high school and being in her last month before her teens started as well. I was happy to hear that Lindsay could spend a good amount of time with her tiny girl.

We'd been chatting for almost an hour before I realised that I was struggling to stay awake. I was starting to worry that I might fall asleep mid-conversation. If I was struggling to keep my eyes open, I imagined that I probably wasn't the only one. If Lindsay had wanted to chat for another two hours, then I would have tried to last the distance, but luckily she had no such stamina, admitting that she was struggling too. We agreed to chat sometime the following day before signing off for the night. I was excited, but cautiously so. I crossed my fingers and toes, which was a pretty childish gesture I suppose, before closing my eyes for the night.

Chapter 14
June 2023 - Continued

Sunday went far too quickly, as they always do. I had been given a little treat to start the day: a lie-in. Max had been so worn out from our beach picnic that he'd slept eleven hours straight. He was a good sleeper and often went through the night, but he was usually awake before 6:30 am, so the extra hour to lie in bed and play on my phone was great.

Once we were up, Mum gave Max his bottle and then played with him before feeding him his breakfast. I headed outside to mow the lawns whilst Rose and Brittany swept and raked the leaves along the outside path. The girls were conscious that we all had to pull our weight in the garden so that Mum's Meniere's didn't flare up again. I felt grateful that I was feeling like my old self again too. After those months of feeling useless, it was invigorating to be able to do the heavy work while Mum hung out with Max.

My niece Ally was staying with Mum for the weekend, so once the lawns, washing, and bathing were all sorted, and once the little man of the house had finally had his morning sleep, we decided to go for a drive to get fish and chips and then go to eat at a park down near the water not far from home.

We had a great time. The girls rode their skateboards and scooters along the path whilst Max had a wonderful time eating chips and watching the world go by while Mum and I talked about Rose's upcoming thirteenth birthday and when we were going to re-book our American holiday, among other things. I hadn't told Mum about Lindsay's offer yet. I was wary about telling anyone in case something went wrong again. I hadn't realised, quite selfishly, that Mum and the girls had been so devastated about Tania no longer being able to help me. I wasn't sure if they thought that she was actually already pregnant, but when I had to tell them what had happened, they'd been confused and upset.

Rose had tearfully asked if Tania was getting to keep our baby. It had reminded me of how young and naive she still was, my girl who'd finally overtaken her nanna in height. She was okay once I explained it and told her that we just needed to find another surrogate. Mum hadn't wanted to upset me any more than I already was, but I could see that she was disappointed and upset too.

I'd been checking my messages sporadically throughout the day. I knew that Lindsay was out. We didn't often talk during the day, but I wanted to make sure I was available to answer any questions she might have. She ended up sending me a couple of links to information she had found about surrogacy, and I checked them immediately but quickly realised that I was on top of everything. I reminded her then to ask me anything she wanted to know. I had researched the subject so much over the previous few months that I was sure there wasn't much that I didn't know, at least in theory.

After a couple of hours at the park, Max was getting pretty grumbly. It was getting close to his nap time, so we packed up. The girls reluctantly helped to get everything into the car so that we could get home for the baby boy's sleep and so I could do some work.

Things had taken off with my podcast, Inked Glam Mumma. What had started as a way to open up about my own traumatic births quickly gained traction, especially since discussing my need for a surrogate. I was partnering with Australian surrogacy and birth trauma organisations and other podcasters who aimed to protect and support women like me. I had already recorded nine episodes, including one with the wonderful Doctor Jack, and, with the help of my producer Darren, I had written another four.

I had found an immediate following. So many women, their partners, and families were living their own similar stories to those I was featuring on my show. The podcast had already attracted a number of advertisers, and the timing was perfect. I had been out of work for several months by that point. I still couldn't believe the company that ghosted me.

I'd seen the would-be bosses viewing my LinkedIn page before they cut contact. By sharing posts about birth trauma and mental health, I had been trying to do something positive. I was desperately trying to heal and wanted to help other women heal. I had every intention of returning to reality, to a nine-to-five job that would require ten-hour days. I was prepared to log on most weekends to finish tender submissions. I had been ready to put my baby into daycare, something I had been dreading, so that I could give my all to my job.

I couldn't help but wonder if a man would have lost a job opportunity for speaking out about an issue he was passionate about. An issue that affected the lives of so many people he knew. I knew the answer, of course, but I decided not to waste my energy worrying about it. I had found something I was so passionate about, and I was helping people in the process. I was doing something I had always wanted to do. I was getting paid to help people. If that company didn't want me to bring the passion I always poured into my work, then that really was their loss.

I sat at my computer that afternoon while Rose and Ally watched a movie. Max was fast asleep in his cot. I noticed that Lindsay had sent through an email with blood test results. She'd mentioned the day before that she had gone and had blood tests to get the all-clear from her doctor. She hadn't wanted to get my hopes up and then find out that she couldn't help. I forwarded the email straight to my fertility specialist. I knew she would want to order a new round of tests since the original ones had been done a while ago, but I figured that it was still worth sending everything I had to my doctor.

The following morning, confident that Lindsay was planning to go ahead with her plan to carry my last baby, I called my clinic. I hoped to speak with the donor team who coordinated surrogacy pregnancies. I spoke with one of the nurses, Sandy, who I had become familiar with when I was going through the process with Tania. Sandy was over the moon to hear my news, jumping straight into action. She needed to review all the medical forms signed with Tania. The forms for blood tests, scans, and the embryo transfer could all be reused with Tania and Brendan's details simply replaced by Lindsay and Cam's since everything had been done electronically. I was thankful that I wouldn't have to completely redo my part of those forms; they were extensive and time-consuming to complete.

We would need to organise new counselling appointments and, of course, all of the legal documents stating that my embryo was being transferred to Lindsay in the hope of achieving a surrogate pregnancy. These needed to be done from scratch. Lindsay would need to make an appointment with my fertility doctor and have a whole new list of blood tests ordered, as well as an ultrasound to check that her body was fit to carry a pregnancy. The tests her GP had sent her for were just the basic STD checks, so many more were required, like a test for endometriosis and, of course, a test to see if Lindsay had the immune issues that I had, namely the Natural Killer cells.

Lindsay had another close friend named Megan who had gone through IVF. At my suggestion, she had coffee with Megan after our picnic. I wanted to make sure Lindsay could talk to someone who had been through the process and ask questions about the negatives of all the blood tests, injections, and scans.

Luckily, my friend was not scared of needles. Lindsay had needed to give herself blood-thinning injections throughout all three of her pregnancies, just as I had done for part of my pregnancy with Max. Those injections were not pleasant at all; in fact, they stung. I was thankful that it wasn't standard practice for my clinic to put their patients on the progesterone in oil (PIO) injections. Those were by far the scariest needles I'd used in all the years I was trying to have Max. The PIO was more commonly used for older women like myself who no longer had a regular cycle. In my case, I had been given them as a precaution because of some heavy bleeding early in the pregnancy caused by a subchorionic-haematoma, a huge blood clot behind the placenta. I was hopeful that Lindsay wouldn't need those rotten things.

By the time I got home from dropping Rose at school that morning, tentative appointments had been booked for Lindsay. She had given me days and times that would suit her, and I worked within those parameters. We were looking at a good six weeks' worth of counselling and tests before, all going well, the cycle could begin. It was surreal. Just two days earlier, I had been starting to wonder if I would have to give up on my dream of trying for another child. I hadn't dreamt of asking Lindsay. When I was going through my network and narrowing my search, she was still pregnant with little Eleanor.

I realised that I'd had an unrealistic expectation when I'd narrowed down that list. I was convinced that one of those four women would definitely say yes. I figured that it would take a couple of months to go through all the legal stuff and tests before they had my little frosty onboard and growing nicely. When I sent that first email to my cousin, I was sure she would come back to me within a few days to say she would help. Being a planner usually served me well, but not always. My initial plan hadn't worked out, but I was cautiously optimistic that things would surely work out this time. They had to. Something deep inside of me told me that this was it. I was going to have the chance to meet my last baby this time.

Chapter 15
July 2023

The next six weeks both dragged and flew by. Rose and her friends had a wonderful afternoon celebrating her thirteenth birthday. The rides and greasy food were flowing nicely just as we'd planned. As it turned out, so were the ice creams and raspberry slushies. The weather had finally turned cold, just as you would expect it to by mid-June. But the sun was out and shining brightly against the dark blue waters of Sydney Harbour. The afternoon went by in a flash. Rose thoroughly enjoyed recounting every moment to her nanna and her boy when we arrived home whilst showing them all the lovely gifts that her friends had given her.

In the meantime, Lindsay had attended all of the appointments that I had booked for her. A few times I had gone along to look after Eleanor whilst my friend was in with the doctor. Each appointment, blood test, and scan was followed by an anxious wait. Because Lindsay was at the top of the age range that my doctor preferred for surrogates, we had to ensure it would be safe for her to go through the whole process. She also had the blood clotting issues that seemed to plague her when she was pregnant with her boys. I wholeheartedly agreed that her well-being was so very important. She had three children that needed her.

I couldn't quite believe it when almost six weeks from the day that Lindsay had offered to carry my last baby, she was given the all clear to go ahead. Every test had come back saying that she was indeed perfectly healthy and able to carry another baby. There were no issues with the counselling; they were confident that the experience would not be at all detrimental to my friend's mental health or to that of her little family. The counsellor had agreed, in fact, that the opposite was true. She felt that two families who were already basically like one would both benefit from the birth of my baby should the embryo transfer be successful . Lindsay and I were already aunts to each other's children. She was one of the few people on this earth, along with her sister Chelsea, who I trusted with my children, and without question, I knew that she felt the same way about me.

We had signed all of the legal paperwork again, all of the same forms that I had already become familiar with earlier that year. All we had to do at that point was wait for Lindsay to be ready for the transfer. I'd never been good at waiting around, I always found it easier to keep busy and so that's what I did. Between the sports and social calendars of the 13-year-old girl of the house, and the ever-increasing needs of a 14-month-old boy, who had finally found his feet I was busy enough. but add to that my podcast, trying to keep my house from looking like a bomb had hit it and helping mum to keep on top of the garden, I managed to keep my mind off the business of getting my last baby happening. Well, at least sometimes.

I found myself wanting to spoil my friend. I wanted to buy her gifts and do anything I could just to say thank you. But I had to be careful. Because of the altruistic surrogacy laws in Australia, gifts could be misconstrued as a form of payment. Even something as simple as dinner or a bunch of flowers could get us in trouble. It was ridiculous and hard because buying gifts and taking my family and friends for meals was how I showed my appreciation. Thankfully, anyone with children would know, there are a million ways you can help a mum without spending a cent, so that's what I did.

I took Lindsay some meals for the chest freezer in the garage. I'm not really known for my cooking, but I had a few dishes up my sleeve. I made a delicious quiche and a pretty good peanut satay chicken among other things. It felt good knowing that, should the transfer work, my friend wouldn't need to try and cook every night if she was feeling tired and sick. I knew all too well how hard it was to care for an older child in that state; I couldn't imagine having a baby and two small children to look after.

I was able to look after Eleanor and Harrison whilst Lindsay was at appointments. We worked it out between us that the appointments would always happen between 10 am and 1 pm. I was still driving Rose to and from school, not quite ready to let my baby catch public transport alone. Lindsay had school drop-off and pick-up as well, and of course, neither of us lived particularly close to my clinic in Bondi. There were probably half a dozen fertility clinics closer to my place, and I'd been to a couple of them to no avail.

I was so thankful when I found the clinic at Bondi. My original doctor there, a tiny woman with a Kiwi accent, was able to diagnose me with endometriosis just from listening to my history. When, that particular diagnosis was confirmed, I'd been so shocked and sad. I had been trying for my second baby for about six years at that point. I had seen four or five different specialists over those six years, and not one of them had half a clue compared with my new doctor. She had actually been through IVF to conceive her youngest child, and so she truly understood what her patients were going through.

I had been seeing my beautiful doctor for quite some time when she left to start her own practice. For a while, I travelled the extra half hour or so to her clinic out West near Hurstville but eventually I'd made the decision, with her blessing, to go back to the Bondi clinic. By that point, I had been made aware of the elevated NK cells and so I'd asked to make an appointment with a senior doctor who would be willing to treat me using an immune protocol before the embryo transfer. I was booked in to see the director of the clinic.

The new doctor was a straight shooter, but she was also sensitive and kind. A combination that I appreciated after everything I had been through. Having conceived Rose naturally on the first try, I could never have dreamed of the heartbreaking journey that trying to have another baby would take me on.

It was such a relief to know that Lindsay would have the same woman treating her .

The tests ordered for Lindsay included the same ones that had identified my elevated Natural Killer (NK) cells. Sure enough, hers were also elevated, though not as much as mine had been. It was no surprise, really. We both had a heap of autoimmune issues. There wasn't a huge amount known about the autoimmune response triggered when a woman had elevated NK cells. I had only found out about my own issues because of a friend who had been having miscarriages for years before finding out about her issues. That friend was the pregnant one I'd been chatting with just after my transfer that resulted in my sweet little Max. My friend had given birth to her little boy, her first child, just weeks later.

Finally, at the start of August, Lindsay was ready to start her medications to begin the transfer cycle. Everything had gone smoothly with the rest of the blood tests and appointments, so the doctor gave her the green light to get started. At first, Cam freaked out about giving his wife an injection. He'd become a little green around the gills, so Lindsay ended up having to do it herself. Having done the blood-thinning injections so many times, she realised that the hormones were a walk in the park compared to those. The needles were much finer and didn't really sting. A minute with an ice pack on the tummy was a trick I'd learned many years earlier, and she agreed that it did the trick of numbing things nicely too.

The next few weeks went surprisingly fast. There were scans every week for the first three weeks and then every three days. The doctor had very precise timing in mind for when the embryo needed to be transferred. It may have seemed excessive, wanting things to be as close to perfect as possible, but the same level of perfection had led to Max finally arriving after so many years. If there was a chance it could work again, then I was so thankful to my doctor and, of course, to my friend for going along with it all.

Chapter 16
August 2023

Friday, 30th August, the day finally arrived. At 9:43 am, bundled up against the cold day outside, Lindsay and I were ushered into treatment room 3. As we walked into the room, I couldn't help but take it as a sign. A sign that baby number three was going to join my family. And Lindsay's family. I was so grateful to my dear friend. I had been included in every possible part of the process. The injections, pills and scans were things I couldn't do despite desperately wishing that I could, but I was invited into such an intimate part of my friend's life. Our friendship had changed over the months since Lindsay had agreed to help me complete my family. We had grown closer than ever, and being in the room that day was an experience I would never forget.

Just as I remembered with my own experience two years earlier, almost to the day, the embryo transfer took less than five minutes. The doctor that we saw throughout the whole process was once again available to do the actual embryo transfer, just as she had with Max. I had forgotten that she didn't believe in using ultrasound to help guide the catheter containing the tiny embryo, microscopic in size, into the uterus . The fertility specialist, a doctor by the name of Jenny Hamilton, was a no-nonsense woman of about sixty. She was direct and straight to the point. On my first meeting with her, I had worried about her bedside manner because she wasn't a big fan of banter, unlike my previous doctor who loved to chat and make me feel at ease.

I had been so worried and confused because every doctor I had seen previously used an ultrasound wand. The nurse would hold the ultrasound wand with that horrible cold gel on your stomach to help the doctor guide the tiny embryo, which was placed in a clear solution inside a long and skinny tube-shaped syringe and inserted through the cervix. I was sure that without the ultrasound wand to guide its way, we would surely lose my little embryo. I had been convinced that it would fall out or somehow end up in the wrong place. Of course, no such thing had happened, and so I wasn't at all concerned about her process the second time around.

Before we knew it, we were back at reception. I had the bill to sort out whilst Lindsay stepped outside to check in with her mum to make sure Harrison and Eleanor were okay. We'd been wished all the luck in the world by several women who worked at the clinic since we'd arrived that morning and indeed over the past few months. I felt so incredibly supported throughout the process of getting pregnant with my little Max and even more so through the surrogacy journey.

One of the nurses came and gave me some written instructions for Lindsay. There was to be no heavy lifting or strenuous exercise for the next week. Because of the fertility drugs, my friend was also under strict instructions not to have sex in the week leading up to and after the transfer just in case she accidentally got pregnant the old-fashioned way. We had a good chuckle when Lindsay read that out to me later. Before leaving, Doctor Hamilton came out, gave me a big hug, and blew Lindsay a kiss through the glass doors that led to the foyer. It occurred to me, not for the first time, what a wonderful woman she was. Every now and then, first impressions were completely wrong, which was definitely the case with the woman who gave me Max.

We walked out of there with the biggest smiles on our faces, not quite believing what we'd just done. It was a strange and completely surreal feeling. My friend may have just gotten pregnant with my baby! The next thing I knew, we were sitting at the same table where I'd had breakfast after my transfer with Max.

We decided that the occasion called for hot chocolates and macaroons. I had always been a superstitious person, so I bought my transfer day treats to take home and share with Mum and kids. If cupcakes had worked last time, then I figured that sharing them might help again. Of course, I knew it was silly. I had done the customary Macca's fries after previous transfers to no avail. But whatever gave a woman hope after a gruelling medical treatment like IVF was at least worth a try.

By 12:30 pm, we had arrived back at my place. Lindsay had driven over that morning after dropping Liam at school. Leaving the two younger kids, Harrison and Eleanor, at home with her mum because she didn't want me to have to drive out to Carlingford and back during peak hour.

After a hundred cuddles from Max and almost as many from me, Lindsay headed home. I hadn't planned to tell my mum and Rose about Lindsay becoming my surrogate, but in the end, Mum had guessed. At first, I had played out a scene in my mind where I'd spring it on the girls once Lindsay was a fair way along in the pregnancy. All the catch-ups at Bondi had been a dead giveaway, though. I had to hand it to her, my mother was always switched on, whether I liked it or not. It reminded me, not for the first time, where my children had inherited at least a good chunk of their intelligence.

By the time I left to pick up Rose from school, it had been four and a half hours since my little frostie, my last little embryo, had been placed ever so carefully into my dear friend's body. I knew that I was going to spend almost every waking moment wondering if that little embryo would implant successfully and grow to become a healthy baby. I wondered if that baby would be a boy or a girl. I had been so excited to learn that Rose was a girl, it meant that I could take my love of pink to the next level. I had always thought that there would be more girls, at least three of them. I'd never imagined myself with a boy, but the moment little Max had been placed in my arms, and long before that, I was converted. I couldn't imagine life without my hundred-mile-an-hour boy. I knew that if I was lucky enough to be blessed with another baby, their sex was absolutely irrelevant.

Within days of the transfer spring sprung. Spectacularly. By the time we hit 6DPT, that is six days past transfer, the chill in the air had been replaced by that wonderful promise of the upcoming summer. And the smell of jasmine in the air which I loved, despite the mild bout of hay fever that it always seemed to bring. The frangipani trees had started to grow the tiniest new shoots that would eventually become new leaves and flowers. In no time, the garden would be filled with the most wonderful aroma, matched only by the fragrant candles that Rose and I loved to collect.

I had given Lindsay a box of home pregnancy tests in case she wanted to go down that path. Plenty of women were capable of holding out and waiting until the blood test which was scheduled for ten days after the transfer. There were other women, like myself, who were impatient and desperate to see those two glorious lines as soon as possible. They would perform test after test, analysing the strips for changes in the depth of colour. Those women were known as POAS addicts, or "pee on a stick addicts.. I had reassured my friend that I would support her decision, whichever path she chose.

It was a long ten days. Lindsay told me that she was too nervous to do one of the home tests in case it was negative. I understood her reasoning. I was devastated when I did that first test with Max. It had been a matter of days after the transfer and far too early for an accurate result. By ten days post-transfer, the embryo would have well and truly burrowed in if it was going to. HCG, the pregnancy hormone, would definitely be detectable by then, at least on a blood test. I knew that the blood test had been done just before 9 am. Lindsay had messaged to let me know that the wait was almost over. My friend had been so disciplined over those ten days. If I'd been the one who'd had the little embryo transferred, I would have done at least five tests by that point. But I wasn't. I had reminded myself many times that my friend had a lot on her plate with her own family and she didn't need me harassing her.

I checked in every day, of course. The meals I'd cooked had been well received by the whole family. It was nice to know that someone appreciated my cooking—my own kids certainly weren't fans. It was a relief to know that I could help keep the freezer stocked if Lindsay needed me to, without breaking the rules. Rose and Max hadn't been too impressed when there was enough left over for their own dinners for a couple of nights. The kids ended up eating Mum's cooking instead, while I happily polished off their shares. The food was delicious—well, maybe not delicious, but it was more than edible. Nevertheless, I was looking forward to doing it again, whether there was a baby growing or not.

By the time I picked Rose up from school at 3:30 pm, my phone had died twice. I'd been obsessively scrolling through my emails and social media accounts all morning, trying unsuccessfully to take my mind off the test results that would be delivered to Lindsay that afternoon. Because of patient confidentiality laws, the clinic wasn't allowed to call me with the test results. I wasn't worried about it, though, because I knew my friend would call as soon as she knew anything.

And she did. At 4:33 pm, just an hour after Rose had jumped in the car, excitedly telling me all about her friend Chloe's birthday party, which was just a few weeks away. I was feeding Max his dinner while Rose finished her homework when I jumped at the sudden ping blasting through the kitchen. I normally had my phone turned down; I couldn't have it switched to silent like I used to, in case Mum needed to contact me or needed an injection. But that morning, I'd turned the phone up for that ever-so-important call to make sure I didn't miss it.

As soon as I hit the green button, I could hear Lindsay crying. My heart sank immediately, but I pushed aside the feeling of sadness and defeat that came over me in that moment. I quickly ushered Rose away from her laptop, asking her to look after her brother for a minute or two. I stepped outside, not wanting my sweet babies to see the sadness wash over me as my dear friend delivered the news I had dreaded.

I asked if she was ok? I tried desperately not to sound sad or disappointed. It wasn't fair to put that on my friend, especially when the disappointment was so fresh. Suddenly she blurted out the words,

"We're pregnant!"

I screamed and then apologised, placing my hand immediately over my mouth. Had I heard her correctly? The kids were staring at me through the glass sliding doors. I hadn't even realised that I had sat down on the table, my feet planted firmly on the bench seat. I had been trying to stop that bad habit for months, but at that moment the table was the last thing on my mind. Lindsay explained that she'd known for a few days. She had managed to resist the temptation to test for the first five days, but on the sixth day, she'd caved. Lindsay had been so desperate to tell me the wonderful news, but she'd worried about the tests being wrong.

It wasn't unheard of for home pregnancy tests to show false positive results, especially during an IVF cycle. The synthetic hormone injections could affect the result. It was even more common to have something called indent lines, which were lines left where the positive line should show up. Except that indent lines were often grey and the result of a faulty test. Then there was the chance of a chemical pregnancy.

In that instance, the tests might show up as positive in the early days and weeks, but the HCG levels were usually extremely low. If you stayed pregnant long enough to get a positive blood test, the doctor would usually be alerted by the low hormone levels. My friend knew about my miscarriages in the past and the months of disappointment that always followed as I tried to get pregnant again. She hadn't wanted to share the life-altering news with me until she was absolutely certain about it.

But there was no need for concern. That day, at exactly four weeks gestation, the HCG level came back at 661. I knew straight away that it was a great start. When I'd received that same call early in my pregnancy with Max, my level had been just 73, which I was told was on the low side. I'd received the news on a Friday. The nurse hadn't been too confident about the viability of my pregnancy, and I had been ordered to re-do the test the following Monday. Of course, the second test had been much more promising, and my little boy then went from strength to strength. It was a relief at that moment to know that the new baby was strong right from the start. Lindsay was excited to confirm that the baby was due on the 19th of May, 2024, just two days after their big brother's second birthday.

Eventually, we ended our call. We were both crying, laughing and so very excited about what lay ahead. I knew there was no way that I could possibly keep the news to myself. Somehow, I had managed to keep it all a secret until that point, but we were having a baby! I needed to tell my girls and Max, even though he wouldn't understand the news.

I pulled my phone back out of my pocket after popping my head in to make sure everyone was okay. I checked the clock on the microwave and was shocked to realise that I had only been on the phone for seven minutes. What a difference a few short minutes could make. I messaged Mum and asked her to come downstairs when she had a minute. Rose was getting worried. I guess you might say that I was a bit frantic. I paced up and down my tiny kitchen whilst reassuring Rose and Max that I was fine. Thankfully, Mum walked in just a couple of minutes after I messaged her.

Once I had everyone's attention, I decided to come straight out with it and tell them that Lindsay was having my baby. My mum had been smart enough, and indeed lucky enough, to have my brothers and me in her twenties. She had never needed to use fertility drugs or any of the dozens of pills and potions I had tried over the years. But she had watched me go through it all so many times. By the time Mum arrived in my kitchen, I had taken Max out of his highchair and placed him into his playpen. Rose had climbed in as she often loved to do. It took her a couple of minutes but finally she realised what I was saying. That our beautiful friend Lindsay was going to carry our baby. The mum of her little kindred spirit, Liam. They had connected from the first time they met when Liam was just a baby. Rose had been so excited then, asking if this meant that she and Max would now have three more siblings as well as the new baby.

I reminded my sweet girl that my friends Lindsay and Chelsea were already as good as sisters to me and so their kids were already basically cousins. Happy with that response, Rose was beside herself with excitement, which in turn got Max going. My little boy was really thriving. He was sixteen months old and could say a lot of words. He was even stringing a few into sentences. There was no way he understood what we were talking about at that moment, but he understood his sister's excitement—that much was clear.

I had no intention of sharing my baby news widely just yet. I had been that woman too many times—sharing the news that I was finally having a baby, only to have to explain to people that I had lost that baby. As if you'd left your precious, longed-for baby in the supermarket or at the park. With each loss, the excitement of seeing those two pink lines became more about what could go wrong. The trauma of those previous losses was never far from the surface. Each time I lost another precious baby, it made it harder to get excited the next time I saw those two lines.

By the time I got pregnant with Max, I had completely lost faith in my ability to carry another baby to term. I only told Mum, Rose, my two nieces Ally and Brittany, and of course, my friends Chelsea and Lindsay. I finally shared the news with my brothers and other friends on my birthday. I was fourteen weeks pregnant and finally starting to feel like maybe, just maybe, things were going to work out.

I was still so very conscious that things could go wrong with my last baby, but there was one more person I wanted to share the news with: Tania. Finding out that Tania could no longer go ahead with carrying my baby because she was already pregnant had been absolutely devastating for me at the time. There were so many mixed emotions—anger, sadness, grief, and so much more. But once those initial feelings had settled, they made way for feelings of love and acceptance, and then joy.

So many people around me had become pregnant over the years while I was desperately trying to get pregnant. It was hard, especially when the pregnancies weren't planned. But I was still happy for the women around me. It wasn't about me, after all. My inability to have a baby didn't mean that the rest of the world had to stop living their lives and having babies.

Chapter 17
September 2023

My friendship with Tania and her little family, whilst different from what we'd initially expected, continued to grow. I was so very thankful that my friend had still come along to Max's birthday party because that day marked the start of our forever friendship. She was no longer my surrogate, but I had still gained a lifelong friend.

I'd really enjoyed seeing Tania get excited about her pregnancy. At first, it had been sad to see that her pregnancy caused her sadness and guilt because of what it meant for me. Of course, I was devastated initially. Her announcement felt like a kick in the gut, as though my last chance of having another baby had been dashed forever.

But I'd always been a firm believer that everything happens for a reason. Just over three weeks after that fateful blood test result came back, Tania went for a dating scan, only to discover that she was expecting twins. By the time she found out she was having two babies, I had already started the process with Lindsay.

The twins were due in early January, but with the combination of twins and Tania's tiny frame, she was likely to meet them at least a month earlier. I hadn't seen her since before Lindsay started her cycle—the one that had just resulted in the positive pregnancy test. I hadn't even told my new friend that Lindsay was going to become my surrogate. I'd always been a superstitious person, and even more so since Tania had gotten pregnant.

Lindsay had also asked me not to let anybody else know, at least until the pregnancy was established. My friend had always been a much more private person than I was, and I respected her wishes. She knew that I had grown close with Tania, despite our little hiccup, so we agreed that Tania was the one exception to that rule, other than my mum, Rose, Max, and my nieces.

It just happened that Tania's baby shower was being held that very weekend, just days after we got the news that my little embryo was growing safely inside of one of my best friends.

The weekend finally arrived after what felt like a month. Lindsay was already starting to feel sick, so I decided that I would tell Tania my news, assuming I could get a minute alone with her.

Tania's family is Italian, and I had never been to a baby shower quite like it before. Her mum, sisters, and sisters-in-law had hired a sailing club with a magnificent view of the Sydney Harbour Bridge. What I assumed would be a few finger sandwiches and cupcakes turned out to be a three-course sit-down meal with a dessert buffet, followed by cake.

I walked into the room not knowing anybody but my friend. It was a bit intimidating at first, but within moments, I had been welcomed into the fold. I found myself seated at a table with several other mums, a couple of whom were also doing it solo, just like I was.

The afternoon was a blast. We played games, took turns having our photos taken with the beautiful mum-to-be, and then watched excitedly as the gifts were opened. Tania had initially planned to keep the babies' sexes a secret, but in the end, she couldn't help herself. She decided she needed to find out and tell the world. It turned out she was having a boy and a girl. There were so many beautiful gifts of clothing and handmade blankets. Rose and I had gone with our usual favourites and chosen some Country Road outfits for the babies. Both of my children had been dressed in sweet little Country Road sweaters from birth, and I always found them to be a popular gift. We'd also had the same sweet little bunnies handmade as the one we had given to little Eleanor at Lindsay's baby shower.

The afternoon ended far too quickly. Before I knew it, I was hugging Tania's beautiful friends and family and thanking them for the invite. Her mum, sisters, and sisters-in-law all knew about her plans to carry my baby. They all hugged and kissed me several times, especially her mum. She told me that my friendship meant so much to Tania, and she was so thankful I hadn't broken off the friendship.

By the time I finally got to say goodbye to Tania, I knew that I had to tell her. I wavered at first, thinking that perhaps her baby shower wasn't the right time, but her mum's love made me realise that my friend deserved to know as soon as possible.

I suspected that she still carried some guilt about not being able to go ahead with our plans. I knew that her babies needed their mummy to be happy and completely at peace, ensuring her love for them was not tainted by guilt.

As I hugged her at the door, I whispered the words she needed to hear: that Lindsay had become my surrogate and we were pregnant. The happy tears in her eyes told me I had just set her free—free of the guilt that had haunted her. I hugged her again and promised to catch up the following week before heading towards the door. I couldn't wait to tell her everything, and even more so, I couldn't wait to meet her two beautiful babies in a few months.

Chapter 18
December 2023

I was no stranger to the surreal experience of growing a child inside of your body. When a baby is wanted, whether planned or not, there's usually a feeling of pure joy and excitement for the future. When you first see those two lines or get that phone call with the blood test results, those feelings take over and they stay with you, growing as your belly does. If you're one of the unlucky majority who experience morning sickness, you may find yourself wondering what on earth you were thinking, intentionally doing something that would make you feel so rotten. Of course, for any woman who has suffered the loss of a pregnancy, the knowledge that feeling sick means the baby is probably doing well makes it bearable.

I had been that woman twice, but I never lost sight of the fact that I had been lucky enough to carry two beautiful, healthy babies into the world. Then, I was so very blessed to have a dear friend carry my third child for me once I was no longer able to do so safely myself. Watching Lindsay grow as my sweet baby grew within her belly was such a humbling experience. But it was hard. I hadn't expected the sadness, jealousy, and even resentment that started to creep in as the weeks turned into months.

At first, I didn't realise why I was feeling so sad. Everything was going well. Lindsay developed mild morning sickness around the six-week mark, and I sprang into action, cooking more meals so she wouldn't need to be in the kitchen when she was feeling horrible. Rose and I would go over once a week. I would clean the bathrooms from top to bottom, while Rose vacuumed and helped get the kids fed and bathed. I also tried to pop in and help at least once a week while Rose was at school, just to do any other little chores that needed doing. Lindsay had tried to object initially but eventually gave in because she felt so tired and sick.

Those early weeks and months were so strange—everything seemed surreal. Deep down, I knew I didn't feel connected. There I was, having a baby, but I wasn't feeling sick. My pants weren't getting tighter, and I wasn't ready for a nap by lunchtime. I wasn't actually pregnant. I knew that I loved my little baby just as I had loved Rose and Max as they grew inside my belly. But it was so different. I found it hard to feel the same connection that I'd felt with my two existing children. I worried that the baby would be born and not want me, that they would somehow know I was an imposter, taking them from the woman who had loved and nurtured them.

All those same feelings I'd had when Max was little, when I was so unwell after his birth, had started to return. I was feeling so ashamed, wondering if I even deserved another beautiful baby. After Max's birth, in my very depressed and traumatised state, I had truly believed that the doctors were intentionally not helping me during those months when my injuries were becoming worse. I had been so sure that I didn't deserve to have my little boy.

I was still taking the antidepressants that my GP had insisted on when Max was just a few months old, so it didn't make sense that I was feeling so negative about everything. I was too embarrassed to tell Lindsay. I didn't want my friend to think I was a jerk. Eventually, I realised that I needed to talk to someone, so on Thursday, 19th December, almost nineteen weeks into my friend's pregnancy, I called my IVF clinic and booked an appointment to speak with a counsellor.

I had secured an appointment for early January. I wasn't surprised to hear that there was no availability until then—it was a week away from Christmas, after all. Thankfully, I received a call the following morning to let me know that there had been a cancellation the following Monday. Someone else had mixed up their dates and cancelled. I wasn't technically the first person on the cancellation list, but the staff, who'd gotten to know me well over the past few years, were concerned when they received my call. I was relieved to know that I was going to be able to talk about how I was feeling. I wanted to try and figure it out so that I could get on with spoiling my loved ones for Christmas and begin the countdown to meeting our new baby a few months later.

The weekend went too fast, as it always did, but also not fast enough. Max had finally learned to fall asleep in his cot during the day, so once he was asleep that Monday morning, I sat down at my laptop. I had half an hour to do some programming for my podcast before I was due to speak with the counsellor.

The podcast that I had started with just a few hundred dollars' worth of equipment in my tiny home office was now being recorded each week in a studio. In the beginning, my focus had been purely on birth injuries and trauma, but I'd branched out into topics like general parenting, IVF, surrogacy, and parenting teenagers.

I felt like I had a wealth of knowledge to share on the topics I was covering, except the teen sessions. I was quickly realising that wrestling crocodiles might have been easier. I was learning a lot on the subject, though, which didn't go astray. Of course, I was still recording sessions where I talked to women who'd experienced birth injuries and trauma. I was constantly shocked and saddened by how many women reached out to me, wanting to talk about what they'd been through during and after childbirth. I took great pride in helping those women find their voices.

At 11:01 am on the dot, my phone lit up. I answered to hear Amanda, one of the two counsellors at my fertility clinic. Amanda was a cheerful woman in her early thirties. I had done my screening sessions with her this time around, including the sessions with Lindsay and Cam.

The receptionist had filled Amanda in on my state of mind but hadn't told her anything more. When she asked what was going on, I blurted it out in a big jumble of words, knowing that

I wasn't making sense. After all, I didn't even understand what I was feeling. I hadn't realised just how much of a mess my mind had become until that moment.

I felt that familiar feeling of shame wash over me as the words left my mouth, but there was a sense of relief as well. I was prepared to be told that I wasn't fit to be that baby's mother—the baby I already loved so much, despite my jumbled thoughts and feelings about everything.

But those words never came. Instead, I was told that my feelings were completely valid, normal, and to be expected. Every woman Amanda had counselled through the process of needing a surrogate to carry their baby had experienced many of the same feelings—feelings of being disconnected from their baby. It was completely normal to feel like a failure and even to feel jealous of your surrogate because they were carrying the baby you should have been carrying. There was no reason to feel ashamed, she assured me. It didn't mean that I wasn't grateful and filled with love for my friend, because I really was—so very much.

"How can I justify taking the baby away from Lindsay? She is growing this baby, and I have done nothing to deserve this," I said as I fought back tears.

"You're wrong," Amanda replied kindly. "You have been through so damn much these last couple of years. Do you know how many people would have given up on having another baby after what you went through last year?"

"I didn't do anything extraordinary, though. Lindsay is the one doing that. I feel like a fake. I feel like I am just being given a baby after doing none of the work."

"I'm really sorry that you feel this way, Tabitha," she responded gently. "We are still learning, along with our patients, about the impact that surrogacy has on all parties. We put so much energy into making sure that the birthing woman is taken care of that we may have neglected our responsibility to take care of the parents-to-be."

I was surprised to learn that some men went through similar emotions when their wives were pregnant. Gay and lesbian couples often felt the same way too, especially in the instance of lesbian couples where one woman had used her eggs while the other woman carried the baby. It hadn't occurred to me for one moment that what I was going through could have been normal. I had been a part of my online surrogacy community for over a year at that point. I had never read about other people feeling the way I did, though. It occurred to me then that, just like the PTSD I'd lived with after Rose's birth and the terrible injuries and trauma I had experienced after Max was born, this was another huge burden that people were carrying alone. It made me sad and angry.

I had been feeling like a bad person, thinking that no one else felt the way I did. I had felt selfish and ungrateful for weeks. I hadn't shared the way I was feeling with a soul because I thought people would think I was a monster. As I admitted these things to Amanda, I wiped the tears from my eyes .

"I really am sorry, Tabitha. You deserve this baby more than anyone I know. We really are still trying to navigate the psychological challenges that surrogacy presents. We deal with only a few cases like yours each year, so you're a bit of a guinea pig." I laughed as she said that. I knew that Rose would have loved the reference too.

The main focus had always been on the surrogate and their wellbeing—the surrogate's partner, if they had one, and their own kids. The process could be confusing for little children in particular, so part of the agreement was that the surrogate and her family would have a check-in with their counsellor at least once a month throughout the pregnancy and for a few months after the baby was born, or as often as they needed it.

However, the intended parent or parents had no such arrangement. Once the initial counselling sessions were completed to ensure that everyone was in a fit state to carry on with the process, the intended family of the new baby was left to their own devices. They had access to the same counselling services as the surrogate and her family, but most were hesitant to book any appointments, just as I had been.

My clinic was starting to realise that intended parents and their families were not getting the emotional support they needed. They were actually in the final stages, I was told, of setting up a new process to make sure that people like me felt comfortable talking about the very same feelings I had been having. I had been beating myself up for weeks, but that half-hour phone call made me realise that what I was feeling was completely normal.

I had sustained injuries that made me unable to carry my baby. I hadn't just decided to do it the easy way and have somebody else carry my baby. Maybe there were celebrities who had done it that way, or maybe there was more to their stories than any of us knew. I was so relieved at that point to finally understand that I deserved to have my new baby. My children deserved to have their baby brother or sister, and my mum deserved so much to have what would, in all likelihood, be her last grandbaby.

The only regret I had about that phone call was that I waited so long to have it. Amanda really helped me change my perspective that day. From that moment on, there was no shame or feelings of jealousy and resentment. I came to understand that those feelings were not at all aimed at Lindsay. If anything, they were aimed at the doctors who had damaged my body and made me unable to do what had come so naturally in the past—carry and give birth to my own baby.

I was more excited than ever after that, especially about the next decision that was weighing on my mind.

Chapter 19
Mid-December 2023

I had been debating whether to find out the gender of my baby. I had found out as early as possible with both Rose and Max, eager to shop and decorate accordingly. In the months of pain and trauma that followed my little boy's birth, I didn't think I would ever see the day when I could use my last little embryo to bring my third and final baby into the world. Then it became a reality on that glorious day back in September, when Lindsay called me in tears to give me that life-changing piece of news. I decided then and there that I didn't want to know my baby's gender until they were born.

I had never been a big fan of surprises, always preferring to know what was coming. My obsessive habit of planning every part of my life meant that I was rarely surprised by anything. Every detail would be meticulously considered and planned for, whether in my personal or professional life.

When I was pregnant with Rose, it had been an excruciatingly long wait to find out if I was having a boy or a girl. I was absolutely overjoyed to learn at my twenty-week scan that I was having a girl. When I finally became pregnant with Max after all those years of fertility treatments, I was sure I was having another girl. I was shocked, terrified, and then so very excited to find out that my second baby was going to be a little boy. That little boy came into our family and within moments had all his girls wrapped around his tiny, sweet, chubby fingers.

I knew as soon as I found out about my last little miracle that it wasn't going to matter what gender they were. For the first time ever, I liked the idea of a surprise. For my last baby, I liked the idea of finding out the moment they were born, and not before. I had started to waver and think that perhaps I should find out so that I could shop, but that call with Amanda changed everything. Lindsay was happy to go along with whatever I wanted to do, even if it meant finding out. But after a while, she started to think that the surprise for everyone would be more exciting. So, at each monthly scan, we eagerly informed the sonographer that we were not finding out what we were having.

Once Lindsay was past the morning sickness—or the all-day and 2 am sickness stage—the months that followed were fairly smooth sailing. During her pregnancies with her two boys, she had developed blood clots in her lungs. There was no explanation for the clots. With Liam, she had gone back and forth for weeks, trying to get answers from the doctors at the hospital where she was planning to give birth. She had been having more and more trouble breathing.

My friend wasn't asthmatic and had never experienced anything like that inability to breathe before her first pregnancy. Eventually, Cam demanded that the doctors do something to help. His insistence paid off just in time. Scans were ordered, and it was discovered that Lindsay's lungs were both full of blood clots. And they weren't small. She ended up needing blood-thinning injections every day until Liam was three months old.

As soon as those two lines appeared again, indicating Lindsay was pregnant with Harrison, she was put straight back on the blood thinners. The blood clots still developed but not to the same extent. After each of her boys' births, she was tested for Factor 5 Leiden. Factor 5, as it's commonly known, is a condition that makes a person more susceptible to developing blood clots than normal. I was familiar with the condition, having discovered that I had it in the early days of my fertility treatments. I had developed clots in my arm and hand after a cannula was inserted incorrectly a few years earlier and ended up on blood thinners for four months until they dissolved. It made no sense to anyone that Lindsay was developing so many clots with no family history or medical explanation.

But something changed when those two lines appeared with baby Eleanor. Once again, the blood thinners were started straight away to try and get on top of the clots before they started. But the clots never developed. Lindsay didn't have the breathing issues she did with the boys. The doctors suspected that the blood thinners had simply stopped any large clots from growing, as they had with Harrison. Everyone was shocked when her routine scans a few months into her pregnancy with Eleanor showed that her lungs were completely free of clots. Whatever had caused the issue in her previous pregnancies had suddenly gone away.

We had discussed Lindsay's history at length during her screening with my clinic. A barrage of tests targeting that particular issue had been ordered, but once again, no cause could be found. My friend was allowed to go ahead with the transfer because of those results and the fact that the issue hadn't reappeared in her most recent pregnancy. And to everyone's relief, at approximately eighteen weeks into the pregnancy, there were no issues when she was carrying my precious baby either.

The absence of clots made Lindsay and I agree that we must surely be having a girl. Baby Powell, or "Stinker Number TWO" as Rose was still calling our baby, was going to even things out once and for all. Between Lindsay, Chelsea, and myself, we had three girls and four boys. We all liked the idea of having symmetry in our little tribe.

I had saved some of the sweet little clothes from when Rose was a baby, and a few things I'd bought on sale at Country Road when I'd been convinced that Max was going to be a girl. I had kept those just in case my last baby was a girl. Lindsay had kept so much of Eleanor's clothing too, hoping she could pass it on to me.

I was so tempted to go shopping for new clothes once I was convinced about my baby's gender, but I stopped myself. It wasn't just because I was guessing about whether my baby was a girl or a boy—it was fear. I had fought so hard to have my little boy and then this new baby.

I had been conditioned, over almost a decade of trying anything and everything to have a baby, to believe that something was bound to go wrong at any moment. I had come to understand that it was a coping mechanism and indeed a trauma response. But I couldn't help it. I believed at my very core that getting carried away and buying things for the baby was asking for trouble.

I had been the same with Max. In the first twelve weeks of my pregnancy, I didn't buy a single thing for my baby. I had gotten excited and rushed out to buy sweet little toys and outfits so many times before, only to end up stuck with the items, not wanting to give them away for fear I might jinx someone else's baby. As dumb as that probably sounds.

Even with Rose, I was cautious. The one exception was books. I have always loved to read. Before I joined the hectic world of parenthood, I would spend every spare minute lost in a book, so I was excited about sharing that love with my first child. By the time I was eight months pregnant with Rose, she had far more books than she did clothes. I ended up racing out a few weeks before she arrived and stocking up on fleecy onesies and singlets. And a pair of pink stone-washed jeans that I simply couldn't resist, wishing that I'd found them in my size as well.

I was hesitant to build the baby furniture too far in advance as well. The sight of me, at thirty-seven weeks, lying on the ground grunting and cursing as I tried to screw the cot together must have been a sight and a half for my poor mum. We laughed about it later, but at the time, it was not fun.

There would be no such challenges with the furniture for my last baby. I had been planning to sell or donate everything once it was no longer needed for Max, after I'd first been given the devastating news that I couldn't carry another baby. Thankfully, I listened to Mum and kept the bassinet. Max was still sleeping in the cot. I had to pinch myself so many times during Lindsay's pregnancy. I wanted to set the bassinet back up the moment we got the news. Of course, I didn't, though. I was waiting until closer to the baby's due date, but mostly because our little three-bedroom granny flat was already full of Rose and Max's toys and other belongings. We had our big yearly clean-out to do over the Christmas break, and then we'd be ready.

Chapter 20
Christmas 2023

And then Christmas week came and went before I knew it. We went along to have photos taken with Santa just like we had done every year since Rose was a baby. I couldn't believe that it had been fourteen years since her first Christmas. Unlike the previous year, though, Max wasn't having a bar of it. Just like his sister at a similar age, my little guy was absolutely terrified of the huge man in the red suit with the crazy facial hair.

It took some coaching and a total act of bribery, with the promise of ice cream afterwards, for Max to finally sit down—albeit on my lap. I had to sit right on the edge of the chair, as far from Santa as we could get without being cropped out of the picture altogether. We got there, though, and in the end, it was simply adorable.

We ended up having pizza and ice cream after the photos before picking up a few things that Mum needed for Christmas lunch and then heading home. Christmas was just a few days later. Some years it was cold and raining, despite being the middle of summer, and other years there would be bushfires raging. There was no such extreme heat the summer that my thirteen-year-old and eighteen-month-old babies screeched and squealed as they found new teddy bears in my bed, where we'd all snuggled up the night before. A bunny for Rose and a dinosaur for Max. The little man of the house was far too young to understand what all the fuss had been about the night before when we'd laid out the Christmas stockings, followed by milk, cookies, and a carrot. But he didn't need to be told twice when Rose took his hand as they hopped out of bed that morning and guided him out to the lounge room.

The squeals of delight as the kids tore into the paper to reveal what Santa had left for them would never get old, I thought to myself. It was crazy to think that there would be another baby the following year. It was going to be pretty squishy on our little rug when there was another little bottom sitting there opening Christmas presents.

And speaking of Christmas presents, we received a call from Liam, Harrison, and Eleanor to say thank you for their matching pyjamas. I had seen the most adorable matching sets online a few weeks earlier and couldn't resist. Rose, Max, and the new baby had the same ones. Once Lindsay and I had spoken for a few minutes and everyone had blown a thousand kisses, except Cam, who just rolled his eyes and laughed before saying goodbye.

A couple of hours later, I gave Rose the honour of reading out a poem she had written about our family expanding. It was interesting to watch how everyone reacted. It was like the gender reveal I had staged on my birthday when I was pregnant with Max. I'd bought a cake from a local bakery, carefully cut a hole in the centre, and filled it with blue lollies before replacing the centrepiece over the top. Mum and the girls were the only ones who knew I was pregnant, so my brothers, Skye, and a few of Michael's schoolmates were extremely confused when the blue lollies spilled out of the centre.

I smiled warmly as Rose read her sweet little poem to share our big surprise with the family.

"Okay, everyone, I have a poem that I want to read out to you all," Rose began. "For a long time, it was just Mum and me. Then baby Max came along, now soon we'll be Mum and three."

"Thanks, baby, that was so beautiful. So, we thought that today would be the perfect time to tell you all that Lindsay is pregnant with my baby. She agreed to be my surrogate, and the baby is due in May." I beamed at Rose before looking around at the confused faces in front of me and watched as, one by one, my family realised what was happening.

I had waited to tell my brothers, thinking it would be a lovely piece of news to share on Christmas Day. Nick and Skye were sad when they realised that they would be overseas for the baby's first few months, but I promised that there would be lots of FaceTime calls during late-night feeds.

The day was over far too soon, as always. Mum, Brittany, and I cleaned up as Rose entertained Max with some of his new toys. I watched them as I tidied the table and thought, for the hundredth time that day, how much I loved my life. I had battled for years to have my little boy. Seeing my children together often reminded me of those struggles and how very worth it he was.

The next week was lovely and mostly relaxing. I continued to cook and clean for Lindsay as often as I could, at least twice a week, and the holiday period was no different. I was ever conscious of the rules around our surrogacy arrangement being altruistic. I had stuck to the rules as well as anyone in my circumstances could have. You might say the birthday present we'd given Lindsay a few months earlier was more than a little bit generous, though. My friend had planned to spend her 40th birthday on beautiful Hamilton Island, three and a half hours north of Sydney by plane, in the picturesque Whitsundays. The trip had to be postponed because she was pregnant with Eleanor at the time. We had been many times before we had kids, and the cocktails were some of the best this side of Maui.

Ever the planners, much like myself, Lindsay and Cam had decided they would take the trip the following year for her birthday instead. Of course, by the following year, she was already pregnant with my little baby, so I wanted to make sure she finally got her birthday trip. I hadn't spent as much as expected on medical bills. I had ended up spending nothing to cover time off work or maternity clothes, so I was able to afford to spoil my friend by booking and paying for her little family to go the following year. I knew it would mean no holiday for my family in 2025, but with a newborn and a toddler in the house, just going to the toilet alone was going to feel like a holiday soon enough.

I thought a lot about Tania as well. We had stayed in touch, and she'd gone on to have twins just a couple of weeks before Christmas, a boy and a girl. The doctors had told her not to pay any attention to the high level of HCG that had been picked up by that fateful blood test back in May. Apparently, it was common enough to have high numbers like that for a singleton pregnancy. She was initially told that she was probably a few months along, but sure enough, her first scan very clearly showed that there were indeed two little babies in there. Amelia and Theo had arrived a few weeks early, on the 25th of November, and both mum and babies were doing well. Tania had offered to go ahead with carrying my baby after the twins were born, but Lindsay had offered to help by then. By the time the twins were born, Tania had met a gay couple who were looking for a surrogate. They'd made six embryos using both of their sperm and were looking for a woman who was willing to carry at least one baby for them. I was glad we'd stayed friends. Our kids got along beautifully, and she and Brendan were truly wonderful human beings.

Chapter 21
New Year's Eve 2023

New Year's finally arrived. Even though we had seen Lindsay, Chelsea, and their kids a few times since Christmas, we decided to have our Christmas party that afternoon. It seemed fitting that we should celebrate the end of 2023 together. We agreed to have everyone over at our place since Lindsay and Cam's home was a bit of a disaster zone due to some backyard renovations they were undertaking.

Lindsay filled us in on her latest news. She had shared the baby news with the rest of their family on Christmas Day. Only Chelsea had known until then. The reaction was much the same as that of my own family—confusion and shock, followed by excitement. They knew that even though the baby was mine, they would get plenty of cuddles. They knew that my baby would be very much a part of their family too.

We had a wonderful afternoon eating and opening gifts. Normally, we would have shared a refreshing spritzer with our salami and cheese, but I was off the booze to support my friend. Luckily, she wasn't a fan of deli meats, so I didn't feel too guilty about enjoying the salami and Swiss cheese on crackers. We had a lovely time toasting the year ahead with lemonade as we watched the kids throw water balloons at each other.

Just after 5 pm, our pizzas arrived. I had ordered our dinner a couple of days earlier from my friend David's restaurant, Attimo. We weren't technically in their delivery zone but they always made an exception for me if I had a function. As I laid the pizzas out on the table, I realised that I had ordered enough food for about twenty people. At least breakfast, lunch, and dinner were sorted for the following day.

I laid out a huge box of glowsticks in a basket for the kids, and once they'd finished eating, Cam and I made them into bracelets and necklaces. Of course, daylight savings meant that the sun was still shining bright, but the kids didn't care. They had a wonderful time playing and watching Cam as he got the fire started.

My mum and I had bought a gorgeous, rustic fire pit during the Covid lockdowns. We had intended to use it every weekend that first winter. It had taken me maybe two attempts to get the fire going before I gave up altogether. Another time, one of my school friends had skilfully lit the fire and we'd all had a fantastic time roasting marshmallows.

I had always considered myself to be an outdoorsy person and very much a boss-babe. I mowed the laws, wielded a chainsaw when trees needed cutting back, and I could do just about anything with my electric drill. There was no IKEA furniture that I couldn't assemble—well, nearly. But that fire pit defeated me every time.

By 8 pm, the babies were starting to fade. The plan had been to play it by ear. If the littlest party animals were up to it, we would go down to Longueville, a five-minute drive away, to watch the first fireworks on the harbour. The fireworks started at 9 pm, though, and it wasn't worth the overtired meltdowns, so we packed everything up and waved our friends off with plenty of time to get the kids in bed and watch the fireworks on TV instead.

As I counted down the minutes to midnight, I thought about the crazy but amazing year we'd had. We had ended things off in the same way we intended to start 2024—surrounded by friends and family, food, love, and happiness. So much happiness. I drifted off to sleep that night, just after midnight, so full of joy and hope for the future. I could never have imagined what was about to happen.

Chapter 22
1ˢᵗ January 2024

My phone always sits on my bedside table when I'm sleeping. My mum had needed injections through the night enough times for me to keep my phone unmuted but still turned down low, so as not to wake the kids. Mum used to say that I could sleep through a rock concert, and I had once, when the band I'd paid to see decided to leave everyone waiting until almost midnight. I was so annoyed and sleepy that I got up and left halfway through their second song.

Becoming a mum had changed my ability to sleep so deeply, regardless of how tired I was. Of course, that wasn't a unique problem for me. Something changes within you when you have children. I had been asleep for about four hours that night, after the New Year's party, when the quiet but distinctive sound of Minions laughing on my phone woke me up.

My first thought was that Mum was having one of her attacks. I grabbed my phone immediately, ready to reply, only to realise that the messages were coming from Lindsay's phone. My heart dropped when I read the words on the screen. Lindsay had woken up with a substantial amount of bleeding. Cam had raced her to the hospital, and they were doing tests to see what was wrong.

Thankfully, the next message—the one that had actually woken me up—said that Lindsay and the baby were both fine, but the bleeding hadn't stopped, and the doctors were running a multitude of tests to try and figure out what was going on. That last message was little comfort, though. In that moment, I was sure, beyond a doubt, that we were going to lose the baby.

Cam had insisted that I stay put at home for the time being. The hospital still had a lot of their Covid protocols in place, and only one person was allowed to be there at one time. Thankfully, Lindsay's youngest sister had been at a friend's place nearby, still celebrating New Year's Eve, but miraculously, she had only had two drinks. She had jumped in an Uber and raced straight over to be there when the kids woke up. Sarah, the youngest of Lindsay's sisters, looked after the kids a couple of times a week, so it was a relief to know that they wouldn't know any better when they woke up to the smell of their aunty making cupcakes that morning.

By the time my children woke up at 7 am, I was showered and ready to leave the house at a moment's notice. I'd heard Mum walking around upstairs an hour earlier and messaged her to let her know what was happening. I hugged my babies even tighter than usual that morning. Rose could sense that something was off, but I didn't want to worry her.

It was obvious that I had been crying. In the hours since being woken by Cam's messages, I had gone through every possible outcome that my anxious mind could think up. Most of the scenes that played out in my head that morning involved complete and unimaginable heartbreak.

I remembered Rose's beautiful poem that she'd read to our family just a week earlier, and it hit me then, like a tonne of bricks. I was angry—angry that I'd let my beautiful eldest child get so excited. She had already ridden a roller coaster of sadness and grief over the years because of my infertility. It hadn't occurred to me during the early years that she could possibly be sad about a baby we hadn't met yet.

But she was sad. I realised it when she started asking Santa for a baby brother or sister. She was four the first time she asked for no toys, just a baby. It had taken seven more visits from Santa before we finally had our miracle boy chaotically tearing wrapping paper from his gifts, far more interested in trying to eat the paper and smack the toys together than actually playing with them—a habit that, even at nineteen months, he was yet to grow out of.

I couldn't believe that my friend, one of the best humans I had ever known, and the precious baby that she was carrying for me, might be in danger. And how would I ever tell my little girl that she might not get a chance to meet our last baby.

At 8:17 am, Cam's message broke through my thoughts and snapped me back to the present. He was heading home to shower and take the kids for a couple of hours. Chelsea was going to look after the kids until they got home, hopefully before dinner. Lindsay had some test results and wanted me to come up to the hospital.

Mum was already downstairs, ready to take over the breakfast shift and so after a dozen hugs and kisses to my sweet, confused daughter and our little Max, I raced out the door and up to the hospital. Twenty minutes later, I arrived at the reception desk of the birth unit where Cam had told me to go.

As I started explaining my visit to the lady behind the desk, I burst into tears. The woman was confused and irritated. She told me over and over that only partners and support people were allowed into the room. In my panicked state, I had forgotten to tell her that Lindsay was carrying my baby. Thank goodness Cam was walking towards the desk, on his way out, when he saw me.

By the time Cam reached the desk, he had heard enough of the conversation to understand what was happening. After a quick word with the woman, I was finally allowed to go down to see Lindsay in room 5.

The moment I walked in, I was struck by how pale my friend was. It made no sense—I had seen her just thirteen hours earlier, and she had been so bronzed and happy, but now she looked so different, so unwell. My heart shattered. I wanted to run from the pain at that moment, but my feet had the courage to continue edging closer to my friend.

In a moment, I was beside her bed. I opened my mouth to speak, but Lindsay beat me to it. With a weary smile, she delivered the news she'd been given just half an hour earlier.

Initially, the doctors were worried there had been a placental abruption, where part or all of the placenta detaches from the walls of the uterus. At only twenty weeks, such a complication would have been catastrophic for the baby. The bleeding was significantly more than anything considered normal at any stage of pregnancy, but urgent scans showed that the placenta was still completely attached.

I had watched *Call the Midwife* enough times to know how serious a complication like that was. I was relieved to learn that there was no issue with the placenta. However, Lindsay explained that one of her blood tests had revealed a discrepancy. According to the tests, her blood clotting factors were out of balance—she had extremely low levels of Factor 8, meaning her blood wasn't able to clot.

It made no sense. Lindsay had been doing daily blood-thinning injections to reduce her risk of developing blood clots again. The doctors suspected that the injections had been prescribed at too high a dose and were responsible for the bleeding. It was a mystery how someone could go from one extreme to the other, but if the diagnosis was correct, it was easy to fix. The blood-thinning injections would need to be stopped immediately. That alone should be enough to stop the bleeding, but the doctors were also going to give her tranexamic acid for a week to help speed up the process. I was familiar with tranexamic acid, as I too had needed to take it when I suddenly started haemorrhaging several weeks after the surgery to fix my prolapse. Lindsay had queried the safety of taking anything during pregnancy, but the doctors assured her it was perfectly safe for the baby.

The doctors had monitored the baby extensively in the hours since Lindsay had first arrived at the hospital. By some miracle, the baby didn't seem to have been affected at all. A scan had shown that the bleeding had come from a small haematoma—the same issue that caused the bleeding I'd experienced early in my pregnancy with Max.

The difference was that my bleed contained large clots that had settled between my placenta and the amniotic sac. But because Lindsay's blood had not been able to clot, hers had presented as a haemorrhage. I had been doing daily blood-thinning injections at the time as well, but mine were only about a third of the strength of Lindsay's.

I was so relieved to learn that Lindsay and my precious baby—our precious baby—were going to be okay. By the time Cam walked back into the room, it was almost midday. Lindsay and I had eaten half a dozen brownies, leftovers from our New Year's party the day before, that I'd chucked in my bag on my way out of the house that morning.

Two of the doctors had been in to see Lindsay just a few minutes earlier to let her know, to our absolute relief, that the second round of blood tests had shown an improvement. The bleeding had slowed down significantly as well, so she should be home within a couple of hours.

By some miracle, my beautiful friend and my last little miracle baby were going to be fine. I hugged my friends as I said goodbye a short time later. I had tried to insist on heading to their place to cook or clean, but Lindsay was so tired, she was keen to cuddle her babies and then just go to bed.

As I drove the short distance home, I felt like I was floating. I had been so terrified that the new year was about to begin in tragedy, but we had been spared. I didn't know for sure who was looking out for us, but I suspected that my beautiful Uncle Greg and the girls' dad, David, were the ones who'd spared us from heartbreak that morning.

Lindsay left the hospital less than an hour after I walked out to head home. By 2 pm that afternoon, she was happily installed in bed, just in time for little Eleanor to snuggle up for her afternoon nap.

I told Rose what had happened once I got home. It was such a relief to be able to explain that the outcome had been positive, that Lindsay and the baby were both fine. My darling daughter hugged me tightly, an act she'd long since grown out of. And my darling little Max—at 19 months of age, he was far too young to understand the sheer gravity of what had transpired that morning, but seeing his mummy and his favourite girl in the world hugging was all he needed to know as he wrapped his sweet little arms around our legs.

A few short minutes later, we were all settled on the couch with our popcorn and leftover pizza to watch the new season of one of our favourite shows. I was almost able to follow along as I kept trying to convince myself, over and over, that things would be okay. They had to be.

Chapter 23
14th January 2024

Lindsay's bleeding continued to taper off and finally stopped on the 8th January. I was so paranoid about feeling Max move when I was pregnant with him that I ended up buying a foetal Doppler—a small handheld device used at home to listen to the baby's heartbeat. One Saturday morning, about halfway through my pregnancy, I realised that I hadn't felt him move for a while. I convinced myself that I'd lost him. In a panic, I booked an emergency ultrasound appointment. Thankfully, everything was fine. Max had apparently just decided that he needed a sleep-in that morning. But it didn't stop me from panicking every time he stayed still for too long.

So, I bought the Doppler. Whenever my little boy slept for too long, and sometimes simply because I wanted to hear him, I would squirt some of the weird cold gel on my belly and search for the sound of his precious little heart beating. I had kept it for my last baby, the baby that my friend was now carrying. When I asked Lindsay if she wanted the Doppler for those panicked moments, she was all for it.

I had seen so many warnings about not using a home Doppler to check your baby's heart rate, but it had given me comfort every time I needed that extra peace of mind. I learned, over and over in my last pregnancy, that the trauma of losing babies never really leaves you. Neither do the stories of friends who had lost babies, even late in pregnancy, where they'd had no issues or warning signs before tragedy struck.

Lindsay was no stranger to loss, and neither was Chelsea, so they both agreed that the Doppler would offer that extra peace of mind. I was glad that I'd kept it.

On the 13th of January, we celebrated my brother Nick's birthday. Lindsay had completely recovered from her scare a couple of weeks earlier, so she was excited to join in the festivities over at Bronte Beach.

The kids thoroughly enjoyed their swim. Even Max was able to have a little paddle in his adorable surfy clothes and shark hat. By the time we headed up the hill to join everyone else for lunch, my little boy had eaten a good chunk of the sand he'd been playing with, despite my best efforts to stop him.

It occurred to me how far I had come since my little boy was tiny. If he'd eaten sand a year earlier, I would have absolutely freaked out, convinced that it would do irreparable damage to his little body. It still wasn't ideal, of course, but I brushed it off as I brushed the sand out of his hair, wondering how on earth he managed to get it under his hat to begin with.

And then the next day, finally, my kids and I got to meet Tania's twins. Layla and Tyler had ended up spending a week in the NICU because, at thirty-five weeks gestation, they were considered to be premature. The babies had weighed just 2.2 kilograms each at birth, which was such a crazy thought. Both of my children had been around 3.8 kilograms when they were born, and even that had seemed tiny at the time.

It was such a relief to see my beautiful friend looking so well. Tania had been able to go ahead with a natural birth for the twins, just as she had done for Isabella and Ava. The twins had come along quickly, especially Layla, who'd almost joined her parents on the side of the road. She had been born within minutes of arriving at the hospital.

Brendan was such a wonderful daddy. He was as smitten with his new babies as he was with his big girls. It was lovely to see. He reminded me of the guy I'd spent several years with in my twenties. I had been too immature to understand what a wonderful husband and father that guy would have been. It wasn't until years later, after several shitty experiences—the worst of which being the guy I'd had Rose with—that I realised what I'd given up with him.

Of course, my path had led me to my two beautiful children, and my last baby that was growing bigger and stronger every day. I wouldn't have changed my life for anything, but I was still glad to see how sweet and supportive Brendan was. Nothing was ever too much for him, even though those two tiny babies had not been part of the plan.

As the afternoon wore on, I became more and more in awe of my friends. Especially Tania. She was just amazing. I had always thought that I was a natural when it came to being a mum, but watching my friend and the way she so expertly and confidently handled her tiny babies, as well as the gentle way she dealt with her older girls, made me suspect that she was so much better at it than me.

Maybe it was the traumatic birth experience that I'd experienced with Rose, and certainly the pain I'd battled for months after Max's birth, had hindered my ability to bond with him for several months. I loved my children dearly but watching how naturally it all came to Tania made me feel a little sad. Looking at her, I couldn't imagine that she had ever had a negative thought or word for her children, or anyone for that matter.

At that moment I wanted her to know how proud I was to be friends with her. I'd felt so welcomed at her baby shower, I really understood that day how important my friendship was to her. I wanted her to know that I felt the same way. As I told her, it took me a moment to realise that she had tears in her eyes.

As soon as I asked her what was wrong, those subtle tears turned to full-blown sobs. In the months I'd known Tania, the only time I'd seen her sad was when she first found out about her pregnancy. I knew that those tears at the time were for me, and my last opportunity, but I didn't dream that there was anything more to it.

But as it turned out, Tania admitted to me that she ended up questioning whether she was going to keep the babies. She and Brendan had been very sure of their plans—they only wanted two children. Their plan had been to move to Canada for five years for Brendan's job. They had planned to help me have my baby, and then if everything had worked out, they would move to Canada six months later.

Finding out that they were having another baby of their own meant they would have to put their plans on hold for a while. It wasn't ideal, but they thought they could figure it out. But then finding out that they were having twins changed everything.

Tania panicked. She worried that all their well-laid plans were completely destroyed. She ended up having a complete meltdown and seriously considered terminating the pregnancy. I was so thankful to hear my friend had sought help from her doctor. After talking extensively about everything, she and Brendan realised that the babies were a miracle and were absolutely meant to join their family.

Of course, there had also been the horrible feelings when she first found out about the babies—the feeling that she was destroying my dreams. I remembered how upset Tania had been when she first told me about her pregnancy. I understood that her feelings had come from a place of regret and concern for me, but I hadn't realised how deep those feelings ran. In my mind, having Tania attend Max's first birthday party, and realising that I was going to be okay and happy for her, had set her free to enjoy her new baby—babies, as it turned out. But it wasn't that simple.

As it turned out, my friend had needed to take medication—the very same antidepressants I had needed for many months when Max was little, to combat the dark thoughts and feelings that had crept into my mind as my injuries worsened.

I realised then that I had put Tania on a pedestal. From the outside, she seemed so perfect and well-adjusted. But in reality, she was just another beautiful and uniquely flawed human being, trying to do the best she could with the cards she had been dealt.

I was glad to hear that she was doing much better and was so in love with her babies, just as much as it appeared from the outside. I jumped up and gave her the biggest bear hug ever. I was relieved to see her tears turn to laughter as I almost knocked her off her chair, thankful that she wasn't holding any of her babies at the time.

By the time my children and I were ready to leave, I'd learnt that not only were Tania and Brendan still planning to brave their Canada adventure—just a couple of years later than planned—but Tania had also built a close relationship with the gay couple she'd connected with while pregnant with the twins.

Tania was so excited to share with me that she had agreed to carry a baby for her new friends, Brad and Simon. She laughed, saying there would be nothing to derail her surrogacy plans this time around, having just had her tubes tied a couple of weeks earlier. Doctors had assured her that she wasn't getting pregnant again—not the old-fashioned way, anyway.

As I drove home, I couldn't help but feel in awe of my beautiful friend. She had been through so much over the previous twelve months, appearing so held together even when she wasn't—a feat I was fairly confident I had not achieved myself. When I had been going through hell and back with my own struggles, I was definitely not held together. I looked every inch the broken woman that I was at the time.

Not only did Tania always look amazing, but she had also managed to come out the other side and help people who needed it. I felt honoured to be friends with such an inspirational woman. I couldn't wait to hear how the next part of her journey would unfold.

By the time Max had been bathed and read two of his favourite bedtime stories, it was only a matter of minutes before he drifted off to sleep. It had been a fun and busy weekend, and my little boy was exhausted. I sat and watched him sleeping in awe, as I often did, still not quite believing that he was actually mine.

And then I remembered the task at hand. I was planning to book a few days away somewhere for the kids and I. We thought it would be fun to book a babymoon. The plan was to go away somewhere over the Easter holidays in mid-April, just a couple of weeks before our baby finally joined our family. But first, I had a few final details to book for Lindsay and Cam's little family getaway.

Chapter 24
February 2024

Before babymoons and belated birthday getaways, though, there was another very special milestone to be celebrated—baby Eleanor's first birthday. The sweet little Valentine's Day baby girl who had stolen everyone's hearts. Eleanor had started walking just before Christmas, much to everyone's delight. Like her brothers and indeed like Rose and Max, she was tall for her age.

Max hadn't been particularly interested in his new friend when they first met. He was only ten months old at the time and such a young baby himself but as the months went on, he started to understand more and more that she was indeed a little person, just like him.

When I finally shared the news of Lindsay's pregnancy—the one with my baby—Max was still very much a baby. Despite his impressive language skills at the time, just a few months earlier, he had processed the news in the most adorable way. My sweet little boy had misunderstood, thinking that Eleanor was actually the baby sister growing in Lindsay's tummy.

Every time Max saw Eleanor after that, he would ask Lindsay if he could cuddle his "sistey." Of course, I'd tried to explain a few more times, but in the end, it was so cute that we decided to leave it. After all, in a way, our children would become siblings of a sort once the last baby joined our families in a matter of months.

Max took his big boy title very seriously, and his big brother title even more so. So when the time came to shop for the little birthday girl's present, he had all kinds of hilarious ideas.

The first gift that we bought, voted on by both Rose and Max, was a toy lawnmower. Max had been given the same one for his first birthday. My mum had given it to him after seeing how excited he would get when I mowed our lawns. It was his favourite toy and apparently a household staple.

The next gift was a rubber ducky family with a huge parent duck and four smaller ducklings that sat on the larger one's back. Max was obsessed with ducks and had the same set at home.

And the third and last gift was initially supposed to be a Spider-Man costume, an outfit that Max didn't own but clearly wanted. Rose and I had explained that Eleanor might like a ballerina outfit, judging by the way she liked to dress up—or indeed the way Lindsay enjoyed dressing her. The suggestion hadn't gone down too well at first, but eventually, we compromised on a tutu and Spider-Man t-shirt. We figured that with two older brothers, it wouldn't hurt to buy Eleanor her own superpower gear.

So off we went, early on the Saturday morning after her actual birthday, the 17th of February, to help set up and celebrate Eleanor's magical fairy birthday.

By the time the other party goers arrived at 2 pm, the kids had helped Chelsea and I to fill balloons, make fairy bread, and ice cupcakes, whilst Cam and one of his mates turned the backyard into a fairy maze with a jumping castle at the end. Lindsay finished the cake and lolly bags with Rose.

Everything looked amazing, and it occurred to me, as it often did, that my friend could easily set up her own party business. Her attention to detail meant that her events were always totally Pinterest-worthy. The food was as tasty as it looked, and I was relieved to see both of my fussy children tucking in, even eating some of my own creations—a rare event for some unknown reason.

By 5 pm, lolly bags had been handed to more than 20 sugar-loaded kids as they and their parents thanked our hosts. Both Max and Eleanor had fallen asleep, so Chelsea and I packed away and washed the dishes. Lindsay had initially tried to object, but she was so exhausted from the hectic afternoon that she'd given in easily, happy to just sit at the kitchen peninsula.

We chatted as we tidied, eating leftover pizza and caramel mud cake as we went. Chelsea talked about the new job she was due to start in just over a week's time. Both sisters had gone into childcare when they left school. They had started with basic qualifications but then studied and gone on to become qualified preschool teachers. They had ended up as co-directors of a centre in Ryde for several years, but one woman at the centre had become unbearable. Lindsay had gotten sick of it and left a couple of years earlier to do Cam's books and some admin instead.

Chelsea was finally leaving to work as the director of a brand-new centre that was due to open a few weeks later. I was thrilled that she'd finally gotten away from the nastiness that had plagued the last place. I had been in that position a few times over the years. There was always a feeling that if you just smiled and got on with your work, things would get better, but of course, that rarely happened. So it was great to see her genuinely excited about work again.

We talked about the kids and how they all wished that the holidays weren't coming to an end. It was crazy to think that Chelsea's daughter, Milly, was already eighteen and finished school. Rose was about to start Year 8, and Chelsea's son, Josh, was about to start high school. Liam, who now considered himself to be one of the big kids, was going into Year 1. We all agreed that it felt like yesterday when it was Mia. Our babies were growing up far too quickly. In just a few weeks, the baby I didn't think I would ever get to meet was going to arrive.

That reminded me—I was excited to share with the girls that Rose and I had chosen the destination for our babymoon. I had toyed with the idea of going to Perth, after Rose and I had tried to go three times during Covid, only to have the borders close each time. Lindsay had tried to reassure me that her Braxton

Hicks contractions had calmed down, but in the end, I decided it was safer to be within a few hours' drive, in case she or Mum needed me to come home.

By the time the babies were up and changed, we had agreed to stay and have an early dinner. The kids had a wonderful time with the leftovers while the adults continued our conversation about holidays and work. Eventually, I realised that Lindsay must surely be exhausted, so I started packing up and urged my kids to get their shoes and whatever other belongings they had deemed essential to bring to a fairy birthday party.

As I popped my head outside, it occurred to me that I hadn't asked about the renovations. Lindsay and Cam had decided to put off their plans to completely gut and extend their house until Eleanor was older. In no time, Lindsay would have given birth, and Eleanor was already a toddler, so I was keen to know when I was finally going to live vicariously through their renovations—even the bad bits.

I loved the little flat I shared with my two, soon-to-be three, children, but it was small. There literally wasn't enough storage space for everyone's clothes and toys. One day, I was planning to knock it down and build us a lovely new duplex with walk-in wardrobes and butler's pantries, with chandeliers on my side and an open slate for Mum to design her side. But even though my podcast was earning me a decent wage, I was nowhere near the point of being able to turn my dream into a reality.

I asked Lindsay whether the plan was still to start in a few months, once she was healed from the caesarean. At first, I didn't notice the way she glanced over at Cam as he cleared away the mess the kids had made. But I did notice the strange look on her face.

Lindsay had looked at Cam, it turned out, to make sure he was okay with her sharing the secret they'd been talking about for several weeks. The building plans were going to be put off for another couple of years.

She and Cam had decided that they wanted to try for another baby. Eleanor was supposed to be their last baby, but carrying another child had made her realise that she wasn't done. Lindsay had brought up the subject at Christmas, and Cam had been immediately onboard. They had faltered when Lindsay thought that she might lose my baby on New Year's Day, agreeing that they couldn't possibly go ahead with trying for another baby after that.

Of course, everything was fine, and so they'd spent hours discussing the pros and cons of having a fourth child. The house wasn't really big enough for everyone as it was, but the kids were already sharing rooms, so one more wasn't going to make much of a difference in that respect. Cam's business was going from strength to strength, so money wasn't going to be an issue.

Lindsay knew that at forty-one, it wasn't going to be easy to get pregnant; she had struggled to get pregnant with Eleanor, and that had been a couple of years earlier. Her doctor had warned her that she may well have passed her window, but she was perfectly fit and healthy, so there was nothing to stop her from trying.

I was so thrilled for my friend, and I was in awe. My friends had made the decision to start trying as soon as they got the all-clear after she'd given birth to my baby. There seemed to be some truth in the belief that you were more fertile in the weeks after giving birth, and so her doctor had suggested they start trying straight after her six-week postpartum check-up.

I thought about the Hamilton Island trip. Lindsay had been pregnant for her last two birthdays, and she'd been so looking forward to drinking cocktails by the pool like we'd done all those years ago. She looked a little sheepish when I first mentioned it, even apologising. As it turned out, Lindsay was now hoping that their little family trip would be their last babymoon.

I hugged my friends then, so excited and full of hope for them and for us. Not only was Lindsay growing, nurturing, and loving my sweet baby, even though she wasn't going to take them home to her family, she was now going to go back and do it again—to finish her own family once and for all.

As I wrangled Rose, Max, and their lolly bags a short time later, I realised that I was going to have to cancel the champagne on arrival that I had organised for the Hamilton Island trip later in the year. I had a few other ideas, though, and I was so excited to think of what lay ahead.

Chapter 25
13th April 2024

I was still in the process of booking everything for Lindsay, Cam, and the kids for their Hamilton Island trip. With the news that they were now hoping to be expecting again by the time they were up there, I needed to change a few of the activities I had planned. I cancelled the champagne on arrival, which thankfully hadn't been paid for in full, as the deposit had been refundable.

I also cancelled the scuba diving lesson that Cam and I had booked as a surprise since it was something Lindsay had always wanted to do. Thankfully, after explaining that the holiday had become a babymoon, the dive company was also willing to refund my deposit. All I had left to do was book the day trip tickets to beautiful Whitehaven Beach, a short catamaran trip from the main jetty at Hamilton Island. Whitehaven Beach was stunning, with some of the whitest silica sand in the world.

Lindsay and I had been there several times before we'd had kids, and I had also been there with my mum when I was pregnant with Rose. It had been my babymoon, and I'd chosen to take my mum instead of what's-his-name. We had a wonderful and relaxing week exploring the island and drinking mocktails.

I couldn't wait to see my friend and her little family enjoy their little birthday—and hopefully pre-baby—getaway. The only thing I expected in return was a million photos.

Planning the trip for Lindsay was what inspired our little babymoon. We hadn't been on a holiday since our trip up to the Gold Coast the previous Easter with my mum and nieces. I had initially invited Mum and the girls on the babymoon, but Mum insisted that the trip should be a special family getaway for me and my babies. Rose and I had gone on all kinds of adventures over the years. We had even been as far as Hawaii and Vanuatu, just the two of us.

And so, with Max's second birthday approaching, I decided that I was indeed ready to take the plunge and go on our first adventure together as a threesome. It would be our first, and last, adventure before we became a family of four.

I was conscious that there was a very real possibility that Lindsay could go into labour early. Her official due date was in mid-May, but she had been scheduled for a caesarean two weeks before that, on 24th April. Once again, she had been having Braxton Hicks contractions. The first time it happened, at twenty-seven weeks, she had woken up convinced that the baby was coming. The pains had lasted for a matter of minutes before going away, but they'd continued, although sporadically, ever since.

Several times over the years, I had looked for holiday destinations within Australia, only to find that it was cheaper to go overseas. That was how we had found ourselves in the US several times, as well as the Vanuatu trip. I would have loved to take my babies somewhere new, or indeed take the whole family on our Florida trip—the one we had cancelled a year earlier—but I was worried about being too far from Lindsay and the baby as her due date drew closer.

When I first had the idea about taking a babymoon, once I realised that it needed to be within driving distance of home, I completely drew a blank when it came to the ideal location. So I enlisted the help of my favourite travel expert, Rose. My girl was excited about helping me find the perfect location, and eventually, after a couple of hours of searching the map and researching the locations she found, she came up with the perfect destination: Jervis Bay.

Jervis Bay is a seaside town about three hours south of Sydney. The bay is known for its stunning white sandy beaches, beautiful marine life, and quaint little shops and cafes. We'd driven down there for a day trip once and were mesmerised by the dolphins playing offshore. I had always wanted to go and stay there, so it seemed like the perfect spot for our pre-baby holiday.

Easter came and went yet again, and this time Max understood what the shiny, foil-covered eggs were. He knew that each new discovery was another opportunity to eat chocolate, so he squealed with delight as Rose led him around the garden with their fluffy bunny baskets that the Easter Bunny had left the previous year. I learned that once girls hit their teens, the Easter Bunny actually brings all sorts of unnecessary cosmetics on top of the mountains of Easter eggs and new pyjamas that he'd always brought. I definitely didn't remember that being the norm when I was a teenager.

The weather was unseasonably hot for mid-April, but the nights were getting a definite chill, so the kids' matching Bluey pyjamas were immediately packed into the main suitcase I was planning to take with us, along with a few days' worth of chocolate. I managed to resist the temptation to pack the tiny Bluey onesie that the Easter Bunny had left for our new baby, instead kissing it before popping it into the wash to get it ready for our sweet baby to wear in a matter of weeks. The tiny 0000 outfit was blue and grey—not ideal for the little girl I was sure was joining our family—but that was okay. There were plenty of Rose's little outfits that I'd already washed and hung in the wardrobe, along with a few of Max's tiny newborn suits that I'd washed, just in case.

By the time I finally loaded what felt like half of our belongings into Mum's SUV a couple of weeks later, the kids and I waved excitedly to her as we drove off on our adventure. We left at 9:30 am, expecting about a three-and-a-half-hour drive, including a toilet break and a snack. Sure enough, at 12:33 pm, we arrived at our destination.

We had managed to book accommodation just a few metres from the sand at Huskisson Beach. Our apartment wasn't quite ready when we arrived so we wandered down to a nearby cafe for lunch, before wandering back along the sand to check into our room.

After excitedly explaining the reason for our holiday to the woman on the front desk, I was thrilled to learn that she had upgraded us to an oceanfront unit. Rose and Max had a wonderful time watching TV and playing with the toy cars Max had found during his Easter egg hunt whilst I unpacked our bags.

Half an hour later, it was time for everyone to get their swimmers on. The beach was just a matter of metres away from our sliding door, but it wasn't patrolled, so I was glad that the pool looked even more amazing than it had in the pictures. Max had been doing swimming lessons for about six months, and he was becoming really confident in the water, but he wasn't ready to swim by himself, so I'd spent more time in the water since my baby had started his lessons, than I had in years. I loved the water but thanks to my birth injuries I hadn't been able to swim the previous summer. I had undergone the prolapse surgery in November, when Max was six months old, and then, between my healing and the bleeding that had lasted almost the whole summer, I had no choice but to sit and watch whenever we headed up to the local pool or had a picnic at Balmoral.

Speaking of picnics, Rose and I had agreed that we didn't want to spend our evenings sitting in fancy restaurants, pub bistros, or even any of the nearby trendy diners that had been recommended to us. We had spent many more nights over the past year on our picnic blanket, whether in the warmth of our house or, in the warmer months, in the backyard. We even pulled out the movie projector and watched a few movies on the fence once the sun had started to set.

So, each night that we were away, we were going to buy dinner from a different shop or from room service, and then we'd have a carpet picnic—or indeed, one night, we were planning to join the other hotel guests for a beach bonfire and have our picnic there.

By the time we had finished swimming and had everyone bathed that first night, I was exhausted. The combination of sun and the long drive had taken its toll. I felt like pizza, and thankfully, the kids were in complete agreement. The room service menu had some good staple pizzas, so we ordered a couple of those and an ice cream each for the kids.

The food arrived just as my phone beeped with a message, so I grabbed my phone as I walked over to answer the door. I glanced at the screen for a second—just long enough to see the name scrawled across the bottom. It was the weirdest feeling, seeing that name there. Kaitlin.

Chapter 26
17th August 2024

The message was from my cousin Kaitlin. I put the phone face down on the side table next to the door as I opened it to collect the trays of food. As I carried the trays, one at a time, into the living area, I realised that my hands were shaking. What the hell was she doing messaging me? It had been over a year and I had not heard back from her. Not a peep.

I hadn't thought about that fateful email in months. The email that I'd sent her, asking her if she would consider becoming my surrogate. It had been such a crazy year. I had met Tania and started the journey with her, only to find out a few weeks later that she was already having a baby—well, babies. I had been so devastated about finding and then losing my surrogate, but then, a little over a week later, my beautiful friend Lindsay had changed everything.

The picnic at Balmoral, just a week after my sweet little Max's first birthday party, was something we had all been looking forward to. My kids and I were excited about seeing our friends at our favourite beach, and the promise of pizza on top of everything else meant it was bound to be a great evening. But I could never have imagined what was going to happen that night.

From the moment Lindsay offered to carry my baby for me, everything moved at a million miles per hour. Of course, it seemed agonisingly slow at the time, but in reality, three months later, my friend was carrying my baby. I had been stretching myself between my family, helping Lindsay, and managing my increasingly popular podcast, which had expanded significantly with the addition of topics like surrogacy, choosing to become a solo parent, and donor conception.

I had also started doing speaking engagements at women's empowerment seminars. I really enjoyed sharing my experiences with other women, and I was planning to do more of it once my new baby was a few months old. I had worked the floor at software conferences for years and never thought I would have the confidence to be one of the presenters. But I was so passionate about helping to empower other women and advocating for them during and after childbirth. I also wanted to raise awareness and educate others about infertility since it was such a significant part of my parenthood journey. I had been asked to talk about the emotional toll that my journey had taken on my life for all those years, and of course, about the book I had written on my birth injuries and trauma. My podcast was taking off, with over 25,000 subscribers.

Each new year comes around so quickly as you get older, and the last one was no exception. One minute we were driving up to the front gate of Rose's new high school, ready to start Year

7, and the next she was helping at the Year 12 graduation dinner, the final school function before the school year was done. To say the last year had been hectic would be an understatement.

I procrastinated for as long as I could—feeding the kids, washing up, and then chugging almost my whole glass of wine—before finally walking over and retrieving my phone from the hall table.

The kids had chosen their movie for the evening, a sweet story about the Easter Bunny. It must have been the tenth time they'd watched it since Easter, but they loved it so much that I didn't mind. As the kids ate the last of their pizza and then started on their ice creams, I finally clicked into my messages to see what kaitlin had to say.

kaitlin had actually sent three separate messages. The first was practically a short story. My cousin explained that her husband, Justin, had been going through her spam folder trying to find a receipt for a cruise holiday deposit they'd paid early the previous year. Before locating the invoice, he recognised my name as the sender of an email received around the same time and opened it, thinking it must have been an invitation to a party or family gathering.

Justin had immediately taken screenshots of my email and sent them to kaitlin, asking his wife if she had seen the email. But she hadn't. The email had been sitting in the limbo world of her spam folder. According to her message, she felt sick when she thought about how hurt and confused I must have been when I hadn't received a reply.

The second message simply said, "I'm SO sorry." The third reiterated that she loved me and asked when we could talk. Relief washed over me as I read and re-read the messages. I had indeed been hurt and confused by the lack of response. I had put so much thought into drafting that email; having it ignored was gut-wrenching at the time. I had tried to convince myself that my letter had ended up in her spam folder, but I didn't believe it for one second.

I started typing a response but then deleted it. After about six or seven attempts, I decided it would make more sense to sleep on it and then talk the following day. I sent a quick note instead, thanking her for the message and asking if we could speak the next day around 4 pm. A thumbs-up and a love heart emoji came back, and that was that. I snuggled up with my babies to watch the cute guy and the cute bunny on the telly.

Day two of our adventures started with a feast of eggs on toast and fruit. The weather forecast was perfect—26°C and sunny—meaning the dolphin adventure I had booked as a last-minute treat would be going ahead.

I had always loved dolphins, so much so that my first tattoo was of not one, but two dolphins. Nick and Skye had bought me a dolphin encounter in Hawaii for my 40th birthday. Rose and I swam, fed, and even danced with a Wolphin, as it turned out. Her name was Kekaimalu, meaning "the peaceful sea." Kekaimalu was half dolphin, half false killer whale.

Spending time in the water with that beautiful creature took my love and appreciation of dolphins to another level, so whenever there was an opportunity to see them, I was there. The boat was due to leave the nearby jetty at 10 am.

We arrived fifteen minutes early, and much to my delight, we managed to get a parking spot almost right in front of the little demountable building that housed the charter company's office. As it turned out, there were only six people on our cruise—the afternoon tour was much more popular with holidaymakers who liked to sleep in.

Once the other people turned up—a couple in their early forties and their eleven-year-old daughter—we were all fitted for life vests. After a quick safety briefing, we were finally on our way. For the next couple of hours, we were lucky enough to see two different pods of dolphins. Our tour guide, Jason, was familiar with all of the animals. Watching the way they responded to his voice was fantastic, and it was hard to believe they were actually wild.

The boat trip went by far too quickly. Rose had been a bit scared about going on a boat after a whale-watching cruise we'd taken the previous winter had ended with almost every passenger, including myself, becoming ill. Thankfully, the calm waters and reassurance from Jason that the trip would be all smooth sailing meant that Rose once again loved boats.

Max had never been on a boat before, but he loved every moment. The wind in his hair, the waves splashing on his little face, and then the funny creatures jumping out of the water and coming right up to the side of the boat—less than a metre away—made him an instant fan.

By the time we stepped back on dry land, it was 12:40 pm, so we headed straight over to the little diner for lunch. Lisa's was a local institution. A couple of friends had told me to go there for lunch—they were renowned for having the best burgers and milkshakes in the bay. Judging by the speed at which my children gobbled everything down, I think it was safe to say they gave it a 10/10 too.

Finally, a few minutes before 3 pm, we walked back into the little beachside unit. The morning and lunchtime adventure had been just that. Max had fallen asleep just a couple of minutes after we jumped back in the car after lunch, so we ended up driving around for well over an hour before finally heading back as he started to stir.

I had spent the morning trying desperately not to think about my cousin. Our adventure had been so much fun, and it had certainly been a great distraction for the most part, but the niggling sense of unease was still there. I hadn't spoken to my cousin for over a year. I'd built her up in my mind to be selfish and thoughtless.

Finding out just the previous night that kaitlin hadn't even seen my email had been strange. I had convinced myself that my cousin was just not interested in helping me and didn't have the decency to tell me. But I was wrong. Somehow, I had to get over a year of hurt and anger.

The kids were happy to put on the TV so I could make a quick call. I dialled nervously, hoping it might go to voicemail. I was keen to push it out until I was back home, but of course, the phone was answered on the second ring. kaitlin sounded anxious, scared even. It was weird. We had known each other since we were small children. We didn't speak or see each other often, but our relationship had always been easy.

As my cousin started to speak, it was clear that she was in tears. I could hear it in her voice, and she was sniffling—that weird sniffling that people do when they cry. I'd been apprehensive about making the call, to say the least, but straight away, I knew she was genuinely devastated. She hadn't ignored the letter I'd poured my heart into. She hadn't maliciously decided to leave me hanging. She'd simply not checked her spam folder, something I too was guilty of.

I hadn't shared anything on social media about Lindsay's pregnancy, or the impending arrival of my third baby. I was superstitious at the best of times, so I had decided to share the news with only a few immediate friends and family. Even my baby shower wasn't going to happen until the baby was eight weeks old. I wanted my new baby here safe and sound, and I wanted Lindsay to be healed and back on her feet before we had the party to celebrate them both.

Because I hadn't shared the news for the world to see, and because I hadn't spoken with kaitlin in over a year, she had no idea that I was actually just a matter of weeks away from meeting the baby that I had initially asked her to carry. My cousin clearly thought that I was still searching for someone to help me.

It was horrible to hear her struggle with that guilt. Without a second thought, I told her my news. I explained that I'd found a surrogate soon after sending her the email. I told kaitlin that when she hadn't responded I'd gone ahead and started the process with Tania. And then I spent the next five minutes going back over everything that had led us to that day, to the little babymoon I was taking with Rose and Max before we welcomed our little baby into our family.

The sense of relief was palpable. I could hear it and sense it, even over the phone. kaitlin admitted that she didn't think she could have done it. Her husband was not at all comfortable with the idea, and she had two jobs and a crazy schedule with her children. I shushed her apologies. It didn't matter now anyway so there was no point in discussing the "what ifs."

Before I knew it, we had been on the phone for an hour. Max had crashed out on his sister's lap within minutes of starting the movie and had just woken up. He was ready for dinner the minute he woke up so I explained that I needed to get everyone sorted out and dinner ordered from somewhere. kaitlin had been making dinner whilst we spoke and needed to get on with things too, so we said our goodbyes, promising to catch up when she was in Sydney in about six weeks' time.

We spoke to Mum that evening before bed, as we did every morning and night. Mum had never gone a day without cuddling her little boy, nor had she gone a day without at least FaceTiming

Rose. No matter where we were in the world it had become customary for us to FaceTime. I told her about my conversation with kaitlin, and she responded saying that she had suspected all along that the email had simply never been seen. We were both glad that what had turned out to be nothing more than a crappy misunderstanding was now all fixed.

The next few days were great fun. We wandered along the pristine beaches, playing with shells and building sandcastles. We saw dolphins twice—both times, they were just metres from the shore. We spent many hours at the hotel pool, shopped in little local stores, and ate in the pubs and cafes within walking distance of our hotel.

I'd become friendly with the brother and sister who owned one of the cafes just a block away, especially Simone, who had given birth to her own little IVF miracle baby fourteen months earlier. The kids and I had gone down to grab burgers and chips for dinner after getting off the phone with Mum that second night, and Simone and I had gotten talking about my children's age gaps.

I often found that people were ashamed to talk about needing help to become pregnant, but it was something I believe should be celebrated. I always loved hearing other people's stories of how they became parents, and I was proud of my own journey, so I loved to share it whenever I was given a chance.

Simone and I had added each other on social media and promised to stay in touch. She and Grant's parents lived in Bondi, just streets away from my brother Nick, and they both spent a fair bit of time up in Sydney. On Wednesday afternoon, the kids and I all agreed that fish and chips, followed by ice creams, would be the perfect dinner, so off we trotted down the road again. Within minutes, Grant had packaged up far too much food, insisting it was on the house since he was off to Sydney the following morning and wouldn't see our lovely faces again.

The compliment definitely put a smile on my face as we headed back towards the hotel. It had been a long time since I'd dated—almost three years. I wasn't sure I would ever want to do so again, but I wasn't immune to a single, good-looking and charming forty-something guy flirting with me. I was still smiling from ear to ear when my phone started ringing.

It took me a moment to notice. Mum had already called and talked to the kids before we headed down to get our dinner and I rarely got calls from anyone else outside of business hours. When I grabbed my phone and looked at the screen, my heart immediately dropped in my chest. It was Cam.

Chapter 27
22ⁿᵈ April 2024

Cam and I had swapped numbers when Lindsay first started her injections. He was worried that they might need my help with the needles. Of course, they'd managed just fine without me. As it turned out, Cam had never actually called me from his number. He'd messaged me from Lindsay's phone at New Year's when we had the scare—when Lindsay woke up with the huge bleed. But that was the only time we had ever communicated over the phone, with the exception of the counselling sessions that had been done via video chat.

So I knew immediately that something urgent was happening. I grabbed my phone out of my bag on the third ring and answered it. Cam sounded frantic. It was hard to keep up with him, but I still got the gist of things pretty quickly.

Lindsay had been having more and more of the Braxton Hicks contractions over the past few days. She hadn't bothered to go back to the hospital because they were not regular, nor were they as painful as she remembered real contractions to be. But everything changed that afternoon.

The boys had been running around the yard, playing with water balloons—one of their favourite activities on a warm day. Lindsay had been sitting on the picnic blanket while Eleanor splashed in her paddle pool within arm's reach, when suddenly Lindsay doubled over in pain.

Thankfully, Cam was inside, fixing one of the kitchen cupboards, and heard his wife scream. By the time he raced outside, the boys were already fussing over her—Liam had wrapped his sister in a towel and was cuddling her while calling for his dad to come and help. The pains had subsided fairly quickly, but Cam called the hospital anyway. The midwife he spoke with suggested that Lindsay should come straight in to get checked.

Once Chelsea had been called to come home from work and stay with the kids, Cam called me. He was just about to get Lindsay down to the car now that Chelsea had arrived. There hadn't been any more pains since the three that followed the one that had caused Lindsay to double over in the yard, but they were still heading to the hospital as a precaution.

Cam and Lindsay didn't want to worry me—they knew the kids and I were away, enjoying our little babymoon—but they wanted to keep me in the loop about everything. The doctors suspected that Lindsay was just having more Braxton Hicks contractions, but because of the extent of the pain, they thought it was best for her to get checked.

By this point, the kids and I were back at the hotel and had started laying our food out on plates. I realised as I grabbed some cups with my spare hand that I was shaking. Things had been going so well since New Year, but there was always a sense of uneasiness. Just as with both of my own pregnancies, the fear that something could go wrong at any moment was always lingering.

We were so close to the finish line. Lindsay was only days away from her scheduled caesarean. Having had three caesarean previously meant that the doctors were not willing to let her go into labour naturally. Doing so could be dangerous. Her caesarean was booked for the following week.

I could hear Chelsea and Lindsay talking in the background and realised that things were hectic enough for them without Cam trying to talk me through everything. Telling him to go and look after Lindsay and get to the hospital safely, I suggested that I would be at the hospital in a few hours. Cam tried to reassure me that things were fine, the kids and I should enjoy our holiday whilst we could. As we ended the call, Cam promised to let me know what was happening once they were at the hospital.

I hung up and looked over at Rose—she had heard enough of the conversation to understand that we needed to get home. In a panic, she jumped up, desperate to start packing. Looking at my daughter, I realised that I needed to calm down. I needed to calm her down. Even Max realised that something was wrong and had started crying. I squeezed my babies tightly, reassuring them that everything was going to be okay.

I quickly formed a plan: Rose and Max would have dinner while I packed all of our bags. Both kids would have a quick bath before I packed the car, and then we would head for home. By 5 pm, we were on our way. Once I had filled the car up with petrol, I hit Mum's name and call button on my steering wheel. My first reaction had been to dial her number after I spoke with Cam, but I realised that she would probably try to talk me out of driving home while I was in that state. By the time I was driving, I had calmed down considerably.

Cam had called again just before we left, letting me know that although the contractions had stopped for the moment, Lindsay was two centimetres dilated, and so the hospital had decided to keep her in overnight. If the contractions started again, she would likely need an emergency caesarean that night or the following morning.

I explained everything to Mum calmly as the kids watched a Disney movie on Rose's iPad and munched on the snacks I'd thrown in her backpack. I could hear the worry in Mum's voice, but thankfully she kept it under control. She knew me well enough to know that I tended to panic about things. She didn't want to get me worked up again while I was driving, so she reminded me to think of the babies in the back of the car and get home safely.

Thankfully, there was no traffic, and we made good time. At 8:15 pm, I pulled into our driveway. Daylight saving had finished a couple of weeks earlier, so Mum had turned the outside lights on for us. I'd spoken with Cam, Chelsea, and Mum at different stages on the journey home.

As I carried Max inside, half asleep in his little Bluey pyjamas, I cursed myself. What was I thinking? How could I go gallivanting off on a holiday when Lindsay was so close to giving birth? I should have been at home. I should've been there, looking after my friend and our little baby.

My house was ready. Of course, I'd spent weeks preparing everything for our new baby. I cleaned the house to within an inch of its life. The bathroom had been bleached and scrubbed to perfection. The kitchen was spotless, just as the loungeroom was.

Rose's little newborn clothes, along with some new pink onesies, had been washed months earlier and then re-washed just before we went away. They were now hanging, ready for our baby to wear once she got home. There were a couple of Max's little onesies folded up ready to wear as well. I figured that putting a few little blue crocodile onesies on a baby girl wasn't the worst thing you could do as a parent. After all, Max had worn a couple of unisex outfits of Roses as well as a cute blue and pink tracksuit that my friend Josephine and her sister had given me.

Oh, and no, we hadn't found out the baby's sex and kept it to ourselves... But Lindsay's blood clotting issues disappearing during her last two pregnancies made us pretty sure—at least 99% sure—that we were expecting another baby girl . Lindsay had never developed those dangerous blood clots she'd had when she was pregnant with her boys.

I felt like it was my fault that Lindsay was having those contractions. I had tried to help her with the house as much as I could. I had spent a whole day the weekend before we left, from 9 am until 4 pm, cleaning and cooking, knowing it would be the last time I'd be able to help until I got back from the holiday. My plan had been to head over the following weekend, just a couple of days before the baby was due, and do another big clean.

Of course, Lindsay and Cam had objected. Cam wasn't one of those useless idiots who did nothing around the house. He was a far better cook than me, even if he was too polite to agree whenever I joked about it. Chelsea had also been doing so much to help, knowing how desperately loved and wanted that baby was and wanting to help in any way that she could.

Almost instinctively, Lindsay rang me at that very moment, just before my thoughts went any further down that rabbit hole. I was relieved to hear her voice. Having spoken with Cam a few times since that first phone call down in Jervis Bay, I was convinced that my friend must have been in too much pain to talk herself. But hearing her calm voice immediately calmed me down as well.

Lindsay and the baby had both been monitored since they arrived at the hospital a few hours earlier. There had been no more painful contractions since the ones that had taken them there in the first place, but Lindsay was definitely in the very early stages of labour. The doctors had been able to stop the contractions, but it looked like the baby was ready to meet us.

I listened carefully as I was given the details. Lindsay would need to stay in the hospital overnight. Assuming that the contractions hadn't started again, she would be allowed to go home in the morning to get her hospital bag and sort the kids out. Lindsay's mum, Chelsea, and their other two sisters were all going to be helping with the kids for the two or three days that she would need to stay in hospital and then for the weeks that she was healing from the caesarean.

Lindsay needed to be back at the hospital at 3 pm, and all being well, baby would be born at about 4 pm. Mum had come down when we arrived home, assuming that I would need to race to the hospital but it looked like there was no need, so once I got off the phone from Lindsay, I insisted that she go upstairs to try and get some sleep. I didn't want Mum stressing herself into one of her Menieres' attacks.

If anything changed throughout the night, Mum would come down and sleep with the kids so I could race to the hospital. But thankfully, there was no urgent call throughout the night. The medication Lindsay was given to stop her contractions had worked. I had intended to stay awake all night, but the stress of the afternoon and the long drive home had really taken it out of me. I managed to keep my eyes open until shortly after midnight.

The following morning, I woke up to the sound of my alarm at 6:40 am. It took me a second to remember everything that had happened the day before. I frantically checked my phone in case there had been updates through the night and was relieved to see there were none. And then it hit me.

If everything went to plan, I was going to meet my new baby in a matter of hours. For the first time since Cam had called me the previous afternoon, I was overcome with excitement and anticipation. The tears that fell silently down my cheeks were the happy kind.

Logically, I had known all along that I was going to have a baby at the end of Lindsay's pregnancy. But emotionally, I'd felt somewhat detached from the whole thing. I knew from speaking with my counsellor that it was a defence mechanism. By not allowing myself to believe that I was once again getting my much-loved and longed-for baby, I could somehow protect my heart should something go wrong.

The sound of my sniffling woke Rose, who had hopped into my bed with Max and I the night before. After assuring my little girl that everything was okay, I quietly got up so as not to wake Max, and headed for the shower.

It was another couple of hours before I finally heard from Lindsay. She sent a text asking if I was up. Max was playing with his dinosaurs while Rose read her latest book. I was almost finished washing up after breakfast, so I dried my hands, grabbed my phone, and asked Rose to play with Max before stepping outside to call Lindsay.

To my relief, she sounded like her usual bright and chirpy self. I realised that I had been holding my breath and finally exhaled, relieved that everything was going according to plan—or at least the new plan. Lindsay was at home, just spending time with her kids. We had gone on enough holidays together for me to know that she had already packed her hospital bag weeks ago, and more sensibly than the bag I had originally packed for my hospital stay when I gave birth to Max almost two years earlier.

There had been no more contractions, so Lindsay was planning to head back to the hospital at about 2:30 pm. I would need to be there an hour later to give me time to be gowned up before being allowed into the theatre.

I felt a bit sad that my mum wouldn't be in the room for the birth of her last grandchild, but of course, things were so different this time around. I wasn't the one giving birth. Birthing a baby is the most intimate and personal experience a woman can go through. Lindsay and Cam had agreed that I should be the support person—a privilege they both believed I deserved—so that I could at least witness my sweet child's birth.

Mum and my kids would head up to meet our baby the following day, all being well. And so, with everything planned and as reality finally started to sink in—that we were just hours away from meeting our special little miracle—I knew that I needed to let Lindsay enjoy the day with her babies.

I had so much to do, but I knew that the house could wait. For the next few hours, I played with my babies, fully aware that we were about to be thrown into the crazy havoc of life with a newborn. I couldn't wait.

Chapter 28
23ʳᵈ April 2024

The day went by so quickly. I wanted to cram as much fun as possible into those few hours, so we went to the park. We ran around like maniacs for over an hour while Mum took photos, eager to capture the moments before three became four. And then little tummies—and even bigger ones—started to grumble.

I was conscious of every moment we had. There wasn't time to drive over to our favourite little Italian place in Northbridge, so I ordered pizzas from a place up the road. The ETA was just 25 minutes, and after a few minutes, I was strapping Max into his car seat.

With the pizzas just minutes away, I put the kids to work setting up a picnic in the lounge room. Knowing that I would be back and forth until it was time to bring the baby home, I ordered enough pizza to last a couple of days, as well as some of the ridiculously expensive ice cream that Rose loved. By the time we sat down to eat, it was 12:48 pm. For the next hour, we sat on the floor, eating pizza and ice cream. The kids had chosen a Disney movie that we all watched. There was far too much excitement and too many questions about the baby to actually pay attention to the movie, but it was a nice backdrop to our last little carpet picnic for three.

And then, suddenly, it was 2 pm. I had an hour before I needed to leave for the hospital. I told Rose to shower and then gave Max a quick tub before getting myself bathed and changed into my comfiest jeans, a long sleeve top, and rose gold cowboy boots. Fully aware that I was probably overdressed for the occasion, I couldn't help but giggle at the thought of how I'd been dressed for the births of my last two children. I realised then that I probably needed to save the full face of makeup for another occasion.

All too soon, and not soon enough, it was time to kiss my babies before heading off. The kids had chosen five more movies that they were planning to watch with Nanna. Mum was amused to learn about the plans for her afternoon but more than happy to go along with it. As I walked out the door, I realised how lucky I was to have my wonderful Mum. Her Meniere's attacks seemed to have completely subsided again.

I was thankful to have her back to her normal, healthy self. I expected things to be a lot easier this time around. There was no chance that my health would be at risk this time—I wasn't the one going through the ordeal of childbirth, after all. But I was still conscious that my mum could only do so much. During Lindsay's pregnancy, I had recorded enough episodes to allow me to take six months off, with the exception of the occasional new guest that was bound to come onto my radar. I was also finally in a position to hire a house cleaner for the first time, for both mine and Mum's homes.

I had found a wonderful team of three sisters who had been recommended to me by my friend Tina. We had done a trial run a couple of weeks earlier and I was thrilled to see how thorough they had been. Both Mum and I would have our kitchens, bathrooms, and vacuuming done once a week. I must have been off in another world, thinking about the lovely clean house that was to come because before I knew it, I was driving into the hospital car park.

Lindsey was in the delivery suite waiting for the anaesthetist to come in and insert her cannula. Cam had gone to grab himself a coffee, walking back into the room, a minute after I arrived. It felt strange, standing there with my dear friend and her husband. They had done everything they could to ensure the safe arrival of that baby, I was intending to take that baby away.

At that moment, I truly believed that my friends read my mind. As Lindsey reached out her hand to me, Cam blurted out, far too loudly,

"Are we ready?" and I couldn't help, but laugh, all feelings of awkwardness were gone in an instant. I wasn't taking their baby, they had been taking care of my baby. Our baby .

The clock struck 4 pm. Finally, the anaesthetist was ready to insert Lindsey's cannula and get her into theatre. I was taken down the hall where I was given scrubs and asked to wait outside. There were five empty seats all in a row, but I couldn't sit down. I was far too nervous and excited about what was to come.

My thoughts drifted as I paced up and down the hallway to the last time I was in an operating theatre about to give birth. I knew I would never get over what had happened that day—the damage those forceps had caused, the pain and distress that followed, and the inability to bond with my little boy. All of it came flooding back. I wanted to run, but I knew this time would be different. My friend had the best obstetrician. Our new doctor, Dr Angeles, was a woman who understood firsthand what it meant to give birth. I knew Lindsay wouldn't be treated the way I had been that day, almost two years earlier, by the doctor who was supposed to deliver Max safely.

Dr Angeles was in her mid-fifties—tall, slim, with a flawless face and long, fiery red hair. We had chosen her together, Lindsay, Cam, and I, because the moment she welcomed us into her office for our first meeting, it was obvious that she had done her research and truly cared. Dr Angeles had given birth five times herself and was completely across both mine and Lindsay's medical histories. She had read up on the details of the deliveries of all five of our children. She had booked Lindsay in, knowing she would be the one delivering my baby. At that first meeting, we were told that she only took holidays for six weeks during the Christmas period and accepted only two new patients per week to ensure she would be available for every one of her patients when the time came to meet their new babies.

As I thought about the wonderful woman who had promised to bring my baby into the world safely, a midwife popped her head around the corner and asked if I would like to head into the room now. And so I did. As I walked towards the door, my strides were long and purposeful. I was on a mission.

It was a strange feeling being in that delivery suite as an observer. I held my hand up to Lindsay, and she took it tightly as Dr Angeles explained each part of the process. I realised that if I sat up too high, I could actually see Lindsay's stomach, so I made a mental note to crouch down. I wanted to be fully immersed in the process but didn't feel the need to see the full extent of what was being done to my friend.

I'd seen enough caesareans on TV to know the process would take only a few minutes, but in reality, it seemed to happen so much more quickly.

A matter of minutes after taking a seat next to my friend, the familiar sight of a pink, squealing little baby being held up in front of us became a reality. I heard the sound of sobbing—a woman's voice. It was a few moments before I realised that the sobbing was coming from my own chest.

I had waited so long, and suddenly, in an instant, that wrinkly little parcel was handed to me, all wrapped up in that familiar striped blanket. The final piece of my heart. My new baby boy. Caleb.

Chapter 29
August 2024

He was perfect. The resemblance to his big brother was undeniable—with his bright blue eyes and his perfectly shaped bald little head. Caleb had the same sweet little round face as both Rose and Max. I may not have been able to carry the sweet little boy within my own body, but there was no denying that he was my baby. I felt the same rush of love that I had felt at the birth of my two older children.

As Lindsay kissed the beautiful little boy that she had brought into the world, I started to sob again. She reached out and clutched my hand. Through my tears, I told her that I didn't know how I would ever thank her for what she had done. She shushed me as Caleb cried and we both laughed. As if he understood the gravity of the situation, Caleb stopped crying and just stared at us both for the longest time.

He was looking from me to Lindsay and back. If I didn't know better, I would have sworn that he knew. It was as though he knew that he was part of something so very special. Every new life is magical and wonderful, but at that moment, I was certain Caleb knew just how miraculous his birth was.

By the time Lindsay was wheeled back to the maternity ward, it was just after 5 pm. Mum, Rose, and Max had met their new baby via FaceTime. It wasn't quite the same as cuddles and kisses in person, but they were all smitten. I knew they had a lifetime of love to give him, and they'd get their chance to show him soon enough.

The next week went by in a blur. Lindsay was able to express plenty of colostrum and then milk. We had agreed that she would do so for a week or two after the baby was born. Caleb stayed in the hospital overnight and then came home. Lindsay ended up going home after three nights. The normal protocol for the hospital where she gave birth was to keep C-section mums in for at least a week, but Lindsay wasn't trying to care for a newborn while she healed. She wasn't being woken up by a baby crying several times a night.

Actually, that's not true. She was being woken at all hours of the night by screaming babies, but they weren't hers. Even though she was in a private room, the nocturnal habits of the babies in the ward were not helping her recovery, either physically or mentally. After the third night, she was going crazy. Lindsay missed her babies and knew that home, with them, was where she needed to be. She needed to be in her own bed with her husband and kids.

Lindsay had been so full of love and happiness when Caleb came into the world, but by that third day, unbeknownst to me at the time, she was starting to feel sad. Lindsay had carried my baby for nine months, feeling him grow and move around in her belly. She had known from day one that she wouldn't be keeping the baby, so her feelings of loss came as a surprise to her. Being surrounded by the sound of newborn babies crying through the night while she tried to recover from her caesarean was just too much. Mum, Chelsea, the kids, and I had all tried to spend as much time around her as possible, and of course, I tried to bring the baby up to see her whenever I could. But those first days and weeks, while she healed, were still so much harder on her than any of us could have imagined. I know that Cam and the kids, as well as the hope in her heart that she was going to have another baby of her own, were what kept her going in those early days.

Caleb was thriving at home. He ended up having breast milk for the first 10 days, thanks to Lindsay's abundant supply. Moving him to formula after that was no trouble at all. I quickly realised that he loved his bottles just as much as his brother and sister had. All three of them had been 53 centimetres long and around 3.8 kilograms at birth, and it often amazed me just how alike they all were in so many ways.

Especially the boys. Rose was such a calm little cucumber as a baby—never fussing or getting into mischief, the perfect little angel. Max and Caleb were completely the opposite. From the moment I heard Caleb's cries when he was born, I knew that I had another little firecracker on my hands.

As the weeks went by, we all settled into life as a family of four. The sleepless nights were brutal, but mid-morning naps in mummy's bed became a highly anticipated event. With Caleb sleeping soundly after his 10 am bottle, Max and I would snuggle up quietly and doze off. Sleeping with my sweet little boy in my arms took me back to the days, after his birth, when I'd suffered so terribly from the pain and trauma of those injuries that had threatened to take away my bond with him.

I began to cherish our naps. At two years of age, Max was still very much a baby, but I knew that he wouldn't be for much longer. I was intent on making the most of every minute of my maternity leave. I was determined to give Max a "do-over." Every afternoon, I loaded the boys into the car to head towards Rose's school for our walk. Mum and I would take turns pushing the pram as we enjoyed the crisp winter air. By the time the school bell rang, we would have everybody back in the car, the boys sleeping soundly in their car seats as their sister hopped in, excited to see her boys and tell them about her day once they woke up.

And we visited Lindsay whenever we could. I knew from the conversations in my surrogacy group that it was important to get the balance right with our visits. I had read about one lady who had carried a baby for her sister. She had breastfed the baby for the first couple of months and was devastated when her sister decided to break that bond. Then there were stories, far too many of them, where the intended parents had not continued the friendship after the baby's birth, as promised.

In those instances, the surrogates felt used. They had been promised some sort of relationship with the child, only to have that baby snatched away the moment the umbilical cord was cut, with all contact ceasing. I knew I needed to be thoughtful and ensure that my dear friend and my beautiful baby would have the kind of relationship they both deserved. Because as much as Caleb was my baby, I could never forget what brought him into this world. I would never forget who had brought him into this world and the sacrifices she had made to do so.

That's why, when baby Caleb was thirteen weeks old—after his sweet little chubby leg was no longer tender from his vaccinations—we finally celebrated our baby shower. The plan was originally to celebrate a few weeks after he arrived, but life with a newborn, a two-year-old, and a busy teenager was a lot crazier than I ever could have imagined.

Between my busy schedule of sleepless nights, taxiing Rose to all sorts of social events, and Lindsay's recovery, we decided to postpone the shower. And we were both glad we did. What had started as a very intimate gathering of our immediate families turned into a huge celebration. I hadn't told many people about my plans to have a surrogate carry my last baby, but once Caleb was born, that all changed.

At first, people were confused when I announced my little boy's birth but the few people that did know were so supportive and loving that I realised something: perhaps everyone would feel the same way. And they did. Everyone began to understand why I had been discussing surrogacy on my podcast. They had assumed that I simply wanted to raise awareness. Some people were sad when they realised that I had actually been going through the very journey that I was talking about with others.

Initially, Lindsay wanted to stay in the background, but her own family convinced her that she deserved to be celebrated too. We did an episode of my podcast together when Caleb was a couple of months old. We had a wonderful heart-to-heart conversation, talking about our individual experiences of the surrogacy journey and how everything was going as baby Caleb grew. After that session, we both agreed that the baby shower should be as epic as our story.

Lindsay was nervous at first. She had never been as outgoing as me. In a way, I guess our personalities are so different that they actually complement each other. I'm the crazy, outgoing joker, and she has always been the sensible, calming force, while her sister Chelsea is somewhere in between the two of us. To kick off the episode, I explained just how epic a guest I had with me that day. I introduced her simply as one of my dearest friends at first.

"Hi everyone, this is Tabitha from the Inked Glam Mumma podcast. Today I have one of my dearest friends, Lindsay, on the show. Lindsay happens to be the amazing woman who carried my third child into the world for me just a few months ago."

I could see just how nervous Lindsay was, and I knew I would need to work a little harder than usual to make her feel comfortable enough to open up and talk with all the microphones and recording equipment in the small studio.

"I wanted to start by telling everyone a little bit about our history. I've shared with you all how lucky I've been to find one of my dearest friends to help me have my last baby. You all know about the injuries that prevented me from realising my dream of welcoming my third child. But for Lindsay's sake, I haven't shared much about her or our friendship," I explained, reaching out and holding my beautiful friend's hand as I spoke.

"I wanted to tell you a story about an adventure that Lindsay and I went on long before we had babies of our own. About twenty years ago, we drove down to Melbourne and then up to stay with one of her school friends in Bendigo. It was a wonderful trip—I won't bore you with all the details—but the thing that's always stuck in my mind about that trip was the day we were due to come home. We walked out to my car to find one of the guys asleep in his swag, under my front tyre." I chuckled at the memory of that morning.

"A swag, for the city people like us, is this sleeping bag thing that country people all carry with them in their utes for when they need to sleep outdoors. Well, it was 5 am when we walked outside. We were keen to get on the road because we wanted to make it back for a Rabbitohs game, of all things. I remember us both standing there, just laughing at the ridiculousness of it, when the guy suddenly jumped up, walked up the hill in just a pair of boxer shorts—despite the freezing temperature—before getting back in the swag and going straight back to sleep."

I saw the twinkle in Lindsay's eye as she remembered that hilarious morning too.

"Oh my goodness," Lindsay exclaimed, laughing as she remembered. "We ended up stuck in traffic and didn't even make it back in time for the game but we laughed for hours about that guy."

"We did, hey," I smiled, recalling that and so many of our other adventures. Every one of our wonderful moments as friends had led us to that studio. I wanted everyone to know what an amazing woman my friend was.

"I am so blessed to have you as a friend, to have had you bring me baby Cay," I said, referring to my youngest son for the sake of his privacy. "We are so blessed to have you."

"You're going to make me cry!" she exclaimed, laughing even as tears rolled down both of our cheeks."

We spent the next half-hour talking about the practical side of our surrogacy journey. We discussed the legalities involved and touched on the need for commercial surrogacy to be legalised in Australia. Lindsay and I were both aware of how rare it was for most Australian intended parents to even find someone willing to carry their baby, let alone go ahead with the process. From the research I had done, I completely agreed with those petitioning to legalise it. Before we finished up, we briefly mentioned the big baby shower we had coming up to formally celebrate both Lindsay and baby Cay with all of our loved ones.

The shower was only a couple of weeks after we recorded our podcast episode, and with all hands on deck and sixty-three women on our guest list, the day finally arrived. There must have been someone smiling down on us that day. We had made the brave—or perhaps foolish—decision to hold a massive lawn party at a nearby bowls club. We stopped short of calling it a carpet picnic. Lindsay, Chelsea, and their little families had well and truly been initiated into our wonderful little tradition, but we decided to keep that as our special thing. We were still trying to capture the same vibe, so Chelsea and I arranged the catering, lawn games, champagne, and favours with a Palm Springs retro theme.

The weather was glorious. Winter had arrived early back in May, just when Caleb was born, but it seemed to have ended early too, much to everyone's relief. By midday, the grass had been transformed with a dozen huge picnic rugs strewn with every cushion that Mum, Chelsea, and I owned. Each rug was set out with buckets of ice, wine glasses, and a selection of chocolates, meats, and cheeses all laid out on serving platters.

There were five different lawn games and a face-painting area at one of the picnic tables. You might think face-painting is only for kids, but imagine glittery painted flamingos, Ziggy Stardust, and palm trees. We set aside a table for the cupcake tower and the main cake, and the last table was reserved for gifts.

I was overwhelmed by the number of gifts piled up on and next to the table. Everyone seemed to have ignored the note on the invite asking them to bring nothing more than themselves and their party spirits. Seeing how many of the parcels were addressed to Lindsay made my heart soar. The love that everyone had for her was wonderful to see and it brought a tear to my eye. When I caught her eye, I could see that she was feeling every ounce of that love as well. I held my hand over my heart before looking away, trying not to ugly cry in front of everyone.

The afternoon was everything we could have wished for and so much more. Having all of the women that we both cherished celebrating little Caleb, and the woman who had done the most selfless thing possible to bring him to me, was magical. Before we knew it, the cake had been shared and goodie bags handed out. One by one, our family and friends took their leave. With their own families to get back to, they congratulated us for the umpteenth time as they left.

Lindsay gave Caleb his bottle as Mum, Rose, and Chelsea helped me sort the presents. Cam had arrived to pick up his tribe and, as usual, he jumped straight into action, helping to clear everything away as he enjoyed a few slices of leftover pizza. Once everything was packed up, I noticed that Cam seemed to be lingering. He was normally all about tidying up as a means to hit the road as quickly as he could.

And that's when I noticed that Lindsay seemed to be doing the same thing. The dreamy, faraway look on her face had been there since she arrived that morning, but it was still there. I had assumed that she was excited and then a bit overwhelmed by the party. I had been so busy mingling and looking after my boys, with Mum and Rose's help, that I'd completely missed it. Like a flash of light, it hit me.

"Do you have something to tell me?" I asked hopefully, beaming from ear to ear. She beamed back. I saw relief wash over her face before she spoke the words.

"I'm pregnant." I thanked the heavens as I hugged her. I couldn't wait to meet that precious new person. It was just as exciting as it was the last time, when it was baby number three.

THE END

www.ingramcontent.com/pod-product-compliance
Lightning Source LLC
Chambersburg PA
CBHW041138110526
44590CB00027B/4058